Whistler

and region

Outdoors

Paul Adam

Cartoons by Tami Knight

Tricouni Press
Vancouver

Canadian Cataloguing in Publication Data

Adam, Paul, 1955 –
  Whistler and region outdoors

  Includes bibliographical references and index.
  ISBN 0-9697601-0-8

  1. Whistler Mountain Region (B.C.) — Guidebooks.
2. Outdoor recreation — British Columbia —
Whistler Mountain Region — Guidebooks.   I. Title.
FC3845.W59A33 1993   917.11'31044   C93-091942-4
F1089.W59A33 1993

Published by Tricouni Press
3649 West 18th Avenue
Vancouver, B.C.
Canada V6S 1B3

Distributed by Gordon Soules Book Publishers Limited
1352-B Marine Drive
West Vancouver, B.C.
Canada V7T 1B5

Edited by Glenn Woodsworth
Designed by Glenn and Joy Woodsworth
Typeset by Joy Woodsworth
Printed and bound in Canada on recycled paper by Hignell Printing

Contents

DEDICATION

This book is dedicated to my parents, Nadine and John Adam, who introduced me to the outdoors at the age of three by taking me camping, then fostered my love of nature before they allowed and encouraged me to start climbing at thirteen,

and Dick Culbert, that demi-god and legend of the Coast Mountains, who not only took the time to teach a thirteen-year-old to climb but more importantly to love the mountains.

ACKNOWLEDGMENTS

This book would not have been possible without the support of a large number of people. Although it is impossible to thank everyone, I would like to thank the following people in particular:

My family and friends, who put up with me while I was working on this project and actively campaigned for me to do lots of field research then encouraged me to double check it.

The people who had to put up with me wearing smelly and sweaty clothes which had been eaten-, slept-, and drunk-in for days, even weeks on end at a range that was far too close for the olfactory sense: in other words my climbing, hiking, and skiing partners.

Glenn Woodsworth, without whose encouragement, prodding, and enthusiasm the project would have faltered, never mind that his experience in writing and editing guidebooks was invaluable in making the book understandable, and his doctorate in geology made sure I didn't confuse quartz diorite with granite, and he did it all while refusing to allow me to buy him a coffee in return.

Joy Woodsworth, who allowed me into her house to visit her husband, then having done so provided me with enough positive feedback that I continued to return until she was volunteered to assist with the editing, and was put in charge of the layout and typesetting by her spouse to whom she is still married. She did at least let me buy her a coffee cup.

Tami Knight, who kept her warped sense of humour on its best behaviour while drawing the cartoons, and allowed me to visit her at home to pass judgment even though I woke up her children, Isaac and Dominique, then ran away with her husband, Bini LeBlanc, to check out the trails.

David Harris, graphic designer and climber, who put in the time required to develop the maps more out of the goodness of his heart than for the goodness of his pocketbook.

Wendy Croft, who made numerous journeys on B.C. Ferries to provide me with the pleasant company I needed to make the walks, hikes, adventures and swims seem less like work and more like pleasure. In addition she politely suggested ways to improve the information in the book and its presentation. As well as she showed incredible patience with my car which broke down more times than was reasonable and only when she was in a hurry to catch the ferry back to the Island so she could go to work the next morning.

Rick Hayes, who walked into my classroom to discuss a student with me, and left with the paddling section and a request to check it for errors.

Kathleen Clarke, who accompanied me on cycling and photography trips, then paid for the beer afterwards.

Michael Down, John Clarke, Alex Gabriel and John Baldwin, who allowed me use their wonderful writings to give this book some literary class.

Robin Barley, Emily Butler, John Clarke and Glenn Woodsworth, who allowed me to use their superb photographs to give you a better feel for some of the trips and activities in the book. The Western Canada Wilderness Committee, Bill Tupper of B.C. Institute of Technology and B.C. Railway generously lent photographs to me for use in the book.

Roger Williams, who checked my physics calculations with the proviso that he get some credit. You may give him credit for any that are wrong.

Darlene Haskins, Paulina Tin, Loree and Gordon Fulton, and Andrea Serink, who sacrificed whole days of their time off so I could check out itsy bitsy pieces of information that only took a few seconds or minutes to actually check. They also had the pleasure of acting as my secretary as I yelled out mileages, directions and names while driving.

The various members of the outdoor community who provided ideas and information but are too numerous to mention.

Nancy and Al Raine, and Anders Ourom, who kindly read the final draft to give me feedback, then went beyond the call of duty to proofread and update it.

The authors of guidebooks, from near and far, whose books provided ideas and information, both directly and indirectly, that will hopefully make this the perfect guidebook.

READ THIS, PLEASE!

This book is only a general guide to the trips described. It is a composite of opinions from many sources and must always be used in conjunction with a full understanding of all risks involved. Persons using this book do so with the understanding that the roads, trails, and routes described here are constantly changing. Although every effort has been made to note real and potential hazards, readers should be prepared for conditions other than those described. Neither the author or publisher is liable or responsible to any person or entity for any loss or damage caused or alleged to be caused directly or indirectly by the information contained in this book.

Introduction

For the casual visitor to a mountain resort such as Whistler or Banff, trying to find out what outdoor recreation activities are available can be frustrating. There are two basic ways for you, the visitor, to get this information. Either you can ask someone (probably another tourist) or you can buy a guidebook or, more likely, guidebooks.

This guidebook gives you a selection of the many outdoor activities available in the Whistler area in a single book at a reasonable cost. If you visit the Whistler area frequently or if your interests are restricted to one or two outdoor activities, I suggest you purchase the appropriate books listed in the Helpful Books section.

As with most guidebooks, this one subscribes to the philosophy that a guidebook is meant to guide you to worthwhile places, not to lead you step by step.

The activities in this book represent a good selection of the outdoor experiences to be found in the Whistler area, but they are by no means the only ones available. However, those described here span the spectrum of outdoor activities available in Whistler and are among the best examples of their kind. More importantly, I hope they will provide you with enjoyment and a good introduction to the area. With this in mind the descriptions are written so as to give you a reason to visit the destination, to help you decide which trips are for you, and to give you enough route and other information to do the trip safely and enjoyably.

The starting points for the trips included in this book are almost all within one hour's drive of Whistler Village. The southern boundary of the Whistler region is, in this book, south of Squamish, and the western boundary is the divide between the Cheakamus and Squamish rivers, which is the height of land directly across from the ski slopes. The northern and eastern boundaries are taken to be the divide that lies east, more or less, of the Pemberton Valley. As the saying goes, there is an exception to every rule, and so there are exceptions to these boundaries. However, the trips outside these boundaries are easily approached from Whistler.

About two-thirds of the activities are within taxi or reasonable hitch-hiking distance of Whistler Village. The remainder start a short distance from the village but are out of taxi range (unless you're rich), nor are they on easy hitchhiking routes.

The introduction to each chapter gives a brief overview of what sorts of activities are available, and the equipment and level of fitness required. It also tells you what assumptions have been made and what information has been left out. Step-by-step route descriptions are unnecessary, either because the routes are self-evident, or else because the routes can only be travelled by experienced parties. Instead, I have supplemented the trail descriptions with comments on the natural and human history of the area to help you pick out the interesting features along the way.

One more thought. Because it is unlikely that you will have time to do all the trips in this book, even in a lifetime of visits, I'd like to suggest something. Make yourself some tea and scones, place them on the coffee table beside the chesterfield. Puff up a pillow or two. Lie down and put your feet on the chesterfield (make sure mother is not watching). Pull the book out and, as you sip on your tea and nibble on the scones, read about some of the trips you haven't done. Then when you have had your fill of tea, scones, and reading lie back and close your eyes. And dream about what might have been and might yet be. Just dream.

Time Estimates

The time estimates given in this book reflect several factors:

- The type of people who will be doing the trip. This means that the times for a walk are proportionally longer for a given distance than those for a strenuous hike, as I've assumed that the average walker (perhaps with small children or not in the best of shape) is less interested in making time than the strong hiker.

- The number of stops you are likely to make because of views, steep slopes, lakes, or anything else that causes you to stop moving.

- A time that will allow at least three-quarters of those doing the trip to complete it within the suggested time without having to rush it.

For example, a fit climber can reach Upper Joffre Lake in a hour but most people will take 2–3 hours. Given that a downhill journey takes about half the time of an uphill hike, I have allowed 5 hours for the round trip, not including time at the top, rather than the 2 hours the climber might take. A fit person, however, will find that 4 hours of travel is plenty of time to accomplish the journey.

Maps

The few maps in this book show the general locations of towns, lakes and main roads in the region. For most trips described here, maps aren't necessary. For many hikes and all treks, proper topographic maps are essential, along with the skills to use them properly. Access routes are always changing in the Whistler area, and most maps are sadly out of date with respect to road and trail information. In some cases approach routes have changed two or three times during the writing of this book.

The topographic maps for this area are available from the Geological Survey of Canada and World Wide Books in Vancouver. The Outdoor Recreation Council of B.C. has published a very nice 1:100 000 scale topographic map of the Whistler area that shows most of the destinations described between these covers. Canoe B.C. publishes a map of the province showing the location of the canoeing and kayaking rivers with some more detailed information. World Wide Books has most in print maps and guidebooks to B.C. The Mountain Equipment Co-op is another good source of guidebooks.

Travel and Safety

It might be the result of the rain-soaked brains that Coast Mountains inhabitants have, but for some reason the guidebooks for this part of the world are laced with a good deal of wit and some wisdom. In the tradition of Dick Culbert and Gordie Smaill, who in the early 1970s set the style and standards for guidebooks to this region, I hope this book gives you some wisdom and perhaps a bit of wit.

> *The Coast Mountains of British Columbia contain some of the least hospitable terrain on earth. Thick bush, foul weather, copious mosquitoes, poor access, fast rivers, extensive glaciation and deep, steep valleys all contribute to their generally unfriendly nature; and many ardent mountain enthusiasts immigrating to this region have quickly decided to change hobbies.*
>
> Dick Culbert, 1974

Those who know and love the Coast Mountains and want to keep them as their own private playground continue to perpetuate the myth that the characteristics described by Culbert still exist in abundance, starting right at the pavement's edge. While Culbert's comment is somewhat tongue-in-cheek, it does contain a great deal of truth. However he fails to mention that it is these qualities that make the Coast Mountains one of our last true wildernesses and provide the challenges and beauty for which they are known and loved.

This is a guidebook, not an instructional manual, but a few notes on special problems are offered below to make your visit safer and more enjoyable. The two most important skills required to travel safely in the Coast Mountains are care and self-reliance. Even on the easiest trip you can be far, in both time and distance, from help. Therefore the first rule of survival is to assume outside help will not be available, because assistance will probably not be able to reach you in time if you have a life-threatening problem. Rule two is to be able to cope on your own with all but the most serious problems. If you are going to do anything other than the easiest hikes, you should have an experienced person in your party. You would also be wise to read an instructional manual designed for our region, such as *Mountaineering, Freedom of the Hills* (see Helpful Books). You can also take course from many outdoor organizations in the province.

Emergencies

In case of an emergency contact the nearest Royal Canadian Mounted Police station. There are RCMP stations in Squamish, Whistler, Pemberton, and Lillooet. In British Columbia, the RCMP has the authority to co-ordinate whatever search and rescue efforts may be required. Before you contact the police, be sure the problem requires assistance beyond your party's capabilities, and then be ready with as much information as possible to assist the rescue effort.

To prevent unnecessary searches for overdue parties, leave notes with a responsible person and in the glove compartment of your car, saying where you are going and when you expect to return. Make sure you indicate other possible plans and routes you might take if for some reason you are unable to follow your original plans. Give yourself a margin of time before having a person declare you overdue. For example, if you are going out on a day hike don't get yourself declared overdue until the next morning, because often searches are in the process of getting started just as the person walks out the woods.

Roads and Vehicles

The roads present more dangers and opportunities to have damage done to life and limb than anything else in this region. All the roads here are mountain roads and subject to hazards such as rockfall, avalanches, sudden washouts, and abrupt edges, both up and down.

The winding and hilly nature of the roads makes other drivers a big hazard. On the winding sections, people have a tendency to cut the corners, so stay as far to your side of the road as possible on corners. The same rule applies on the crests of hills. As dangerous as the paved roads are, the gravel ones are more so as they tend to be extra winding, hillier, and narrower. Remember that on gravel a car handles in much the same way it does on ice.

When driving on a dusty gravel road, drive with your headlights on and stay well behind any vehicles in front of you. If you are travelling slowly stop and let the vehicles behind you pass.

Watch closely for logging trucks on back roads. Some logging truck drivers feel that they own the gravel roads and forget that other vehicles have the right to use these roads. Logging trucks are not very manoeuvrable nor easy to handle, so that while a car can make a sudden correction the logging truck cannot, which means it is up to you to avoid a collision even if you are not at fault.

Snow and ice make travel even more dangerous and require that you pay more attention than usual. Driving is easier and safer, and better progress is made if you travel at a slow and steady rate.

Here are a few tips and items to carry that you'll be glad you have if you have car trouble.

A full tank of gas is enough for any trip described in this book. Make sure your spare tire has air in it.

Carry your own jumper cables and tow rope, because in the back of beyond people are always willing to give you a boost or a tow but chances are they won't have the equipment needed. A good bumper jack not only allows you to change tires quickly in the rain but comes in handy for getting out of ditches and icy, muddy ruts. An air pump that operates off your cigarette lighter is handy for pumping up your flat spare tire.

Carry a litre of oil just in case you need it and a 2 litre or larger container to pack water for your radiator. It's nice to have a towel to dry off with after changing a tire in the rain, or just to lie on instead of the wet ground, or in case you see a nice place to swim.

When parking in the middle of nowhere, park facing downhill, preferably in the direction you want to go. This allows you to jump-start your car if it quits, and in winter it means at you can least start driving home on the snowy road. Put a rock under your wheel to prevent the car from rolling if the emergency brake fails while you are away.

Don't leave valuables in your car. If you must, lock them in the trunk.

In winter, good winter tires, chains and a snow shovel are required. The first two not only help you get places but prevent you from being a hazard to others. The latter not only digs you out of snowbanks but gets you back on the main roads after snowplows have thrown up a wall of snow blocking your exit from a side road. Be careful in winter that you don't get snowed-in or avalanched-in up a logging road or you will find yourself short a car until the late spring.

Equipment and Clothing

Because this book covers so many outdoor activities, I assume that you will pick trips that are within your level of fitness, skill, and experience. The introduction to each chapter indicates the type of experience you should have had before attempting the activities, and the absolute minimum amount of gear needed.

There are many good manuals and pamphlets that outline the gear needed for particular types of trips. That said, there is no teacher like experience. Two general pointers for the inexperienced outdoors person: don't over-equip yourself with gear that you don't know how to use, and start with the easier activities and work up.

For hikers, a good set of footwear, something appropriately sturdy and with a non-slip sole, is mandatory for all trips, because many accidents result from poor footwear. Because of the general wetness of the area the more waterproof your footwear the drier your feet will stay. It is amazing how damp the area is even after a long dry spell.

On trips where you are likely to get your feet wet, a pair of old low-cut runners and nylon shorts will help keep your boots and clothing dry. When fording rivers or having to get out of a boat and into the water, put the runners and shorts on and do your thing then towel off and put your original gear back on. The runners are also handy around camp while your boots are drying. Although at first sight it seems idiotic to hike in your underwear (shorts if you are modest), there is a measure of sanity to it. Upon arriving at your destination and towelling off you can put on dry clothes and not have to worry about drying anything or packing a third set of clothes. A small towel and plenty of socks and gloves will save you from damp-induced hypothermia. If you put your clothes in a plastic bag within a pack, the clothes will remain dry through the severest storm and even a decent dunking.

The general wetness of the climate makes clothing and sleeping bags made from synthetic fibres preferable to those of down. Synthetics not only dry faster and have better heat retaining properties when wet, but it is seldom cold enough to justify the extra expense of down. In wet weather, Gore-tex coats, overmitts, and gaiters more than repay their cost by keeping everything underneath as dry as can be expected.

For mountain bikers, helmets are essential not only to prevent injury from a crash but to prevent it when a low-hanging branch surprises you.

For boaters, a life jacket is essential on any water. It *must* be worn, as it does not do you any good lying in the bottom of the boat. Helmets and wet suits are essential on any fast-moving water. A change of clothes in a plastic bag and a thermos of hot drink are needed on any major paddle.

Many people keep a set of dry clothes, a towel, and a stove in the car so they can warm up after the trip.

Weather

Storms can blow in quickly, even in summer. On any trip of more than a couple of hours, take rainwear and warm clothing. If you are on a short trip without bad-weather gear, turn back when you see a storm moving in. Even during spells of good weather there are so many microclimates in the mountains that you must be prepared for major clothing changes. If your trip is more than one day in length, be prepared to travel in bad weather and limited visibility.

Water

If you are doing anything in, on, or near the water remember that all the lakes and streams in the Whistler area are snow- or glacier-fed. Even after the longest hot spell they tend to be cold, often extremely so. With this in mind always carry a towel and some extra clothes.

Mountain streams are characterized by steep drops, rocky bottoms, and rapid changes in water level. A hot spell or heavy rain results in a rapid rise in the water level. Trees can span, hang over, or lie in the water, creating a hazard that can have fatal consequences.

Not long ago, almost any water in the Whistler region was safe to drink. Sadly, this is changing. Increasing population and use of the back country and the slow spread of the water-borne parasitic disease giardia make drinking the water a bit of a gamble. Many people still drink any water that they find; others drink only water that they have brought from home or that they treat themselves. In general, the farther from civilization and the higher in elevation you are, the safer the water is likely to be. Lakes and rivers near glaciers contain much glacial silt, which gives the water a crunchy taste, but if you let it settle and then decant it, the water is very good.

Vegetation

In addition to its old-growth forests, the Coast Mountains are renowned for thick underbrush that can slow off-trail travel to a crawl. For this reason it is better to travel a route you know than one you don't, as they say the better the devil you know than the one you don't. In general, ridges offer better travel than narrow valley bottoms. Unlogged forest appears relatively dark green when seen from a distance and offers generally good walking. Relatively light green vegetation tends to be extremely thick underbrush or overgrown logging slash: avoid such areas unless you have great quantities of time and energy. Thick bush, in addition to being very difficult to travel through, restricts your visibility and can hide short drops, rocks, and holes.

Ethics

Take nothing but photographs; leave nothing but footprints.

Spelunker's motto

This saying has become the dictum for those who pursue wilderness recreation. The objective is to leave the wilderness in the same state you found it so that no one knows you passed through the area.

We have an unfortunate habit of separating ourselves and our actions from the rest of nature without realizing we are a component of nature. Most animals, and man is an animal, take from nature only what they need and can use at the time. Unfortunately we frequently fail to do this. Consequently not only is our survival as a species threatened, but also that of many other species vital to our survival. *Please think of the future and do the least possible damage to the environment as you travel through it.*

If an action such as walking across an alpine meadow results in substantial damage to the environment, it may be better to totally damage one small area rather than to substantially damage a large area. For example, one person walking across a meadow does a fair amount of damage. It might be better for the next nine people to follow the same path and completely destroy one set of flowers rather than to find their own paths and severely damage an additional nine sets of flowers by finding their own paths across the meadow. *Please walk in the footprints of those who preceded you and nowhere else.*

Finally, whatever you take in with you, bring out with you. Pack it, wear it, eat it, or get it to walk out but *get it out.* Anything burnt, buried, or otherwise left behind is dangerous to the health of both animals and environment. Where there are pit toilets use them; if there aren't any, bury or cover your wastes where they can't be seen, and well away from any water supply. *If you pack it in, then pack it out.*

Fires

> With loss of wilderness and more intense use of the alpine areas it is
> necessary that people drop their vestige 'frontier' attitudes on weekend
> trips from Vancouver. The first thing to be thrown out should be the
> hatchet. . . . Axes are pretty well useless on recreational outings and a
> sign of the romantic novice. . . . One kid with an ax and scout manual
> can cause more permanent damage at timberline than an entire
> 50-member herd from a hiking club.
>
> Dick Culbert, 1974

Culbert is absolutely right in his comment about the axe and in the
implicit comments about fires that go with it. The use of an axe to gather
wood for shelter and fuel was largely abandoned many years ago with the
development of lightweight tents and stoves. Today, unless you have
somehow lost your tent, there is no reason to build a shelter from tree
boughs. As for the use of wood for fuel, unless you have lost your stove
or run out of gas, a stove will cook your dinner faster.

Today there is only one reason that requires you build a fire: the need to prevent hypothermia when everything is cold and wet and a fire is the only way of drying out and warming up. If you must have a fire, use dead branches only, if for no other reason than they are easier to light and burn better. Even dead wood has an ecological role, especially in alpine environments, so minimize your use of it. And only use it if there is lots of water around so you can properly put the fire out. Before you start to build your fire, scrape the organic layer away to reach the mineral soil, then soak the soil to prevent any organic matter that remains from burning. Keep the fire low and don't let it get too hot. When you put it out, soak the large logs individually, the fire and ashes, and the surrounding area, and then throw on some more water just to make doubly sure. Fill the firepit in with dirt so that nature can begin to heal the scar.

As for campfires for pleasure in the evening, have them only if you are in areas such as campgrounds where wood is supplied for that purpose.

Multiple Use

One of the joys and problems of the outdoors is there are essentially no rules and you can do more or less as you please. Because there is a finite amount of wilderness and an increasing number of people using it in an increasing number of ways, there is bound to be conflict. This conflict can be minimized by respecting the needs and requirements of others. This can be done by a certain amount of compartmentalization and common environmental sense. Compartmentalization occurs – it need not be officially mandated – where it is recognized that a certain activity occurs within an area, and if you do not wish to encounter that activity, you stay out of the area. A great example of this occurs in the Rutherford Creek valley. There, members of the Pemberton Snowmobile Club use the logging road and a trail they have developed to get to the Pemberton Icefield via the Snekwnukwa7 Glacier. If you as a cross-country skier do not like the sight and sound of snowmobiles, then stay away from this area, as the snowmobilers here are staying away from other areas so that they do not bother skiers.

Using environmental common sense and leaving the backcountry with the fewest possible traces of your passage will help prevent the development of bad feelings by other groups towards you and your activity. It takes only one person trashing the environment once to give your sport a bad name. Unfortunately, activities that involve technological developments, including snowmobiling and mountain biking, bear the brunt of such attacks. But when they are done properly, they have no greater environmental impact than many traditional activities. Hikers frequently get upset at mountain bikers but seldom at horses, yet horses do considerably more damage to a trail. In an area such as Whistler where there are a variety of activities, respect the needs and desires of others. This way the wilderness will remain open to all, with the fewest possible regulations.

Natural Features

The Whistler region is in many ways a product of its geology, including the effects of the last ice age and recent volcanic activity, of its geography, and its climate, which is strongly affected by its proximity to the ocean.

Geology, Geography, & Climate

The Coast Mountains are part of the "Rim of Fire" that encircles the Pacific Ocean. But the mountains weren't always here. Some 200 million years ago the western edge of North America was in the centre of the province. The area to the west had either not formed yet, or lay elsewhere, perhaps at the latitude of southern California. Since that time, much of the floor of the Pacific Ocean has been driven beneath North America, adding bits and pieces to the continent's western edge. Where the ocean crust dives beneath the continent, heat is produced and rocks deep in the earth melt. This molten rock, or magma, is injected beneath the surface to form the granite family of rocks (beloved by rock climbers on the Squamish Chief) or erupts as volcanoes (such as Mt. Meager or Mt. Garibaldi). The present mountains were formed about 50 million years ago by forces that squeezed and uplifted the new additions to the continent.

Mt. Garibaldi, The Black Tusk, and Mt. Meager were formed by (geologically) recent volcanic activity. These mountains are volcanoes that are an extension of the Cascade mountain chain that includes Shasta, St. Helens, Rainier, and Baker. The Mt. Garibaldi area had extensive volcanic activity about 10–12 000 years ago, when the region was just emerging from the last ice age. The Barrier, near Black Tusk, is a classic example of where magma and ice met. Here the hot lava from an eruption near Mt. Garibaldi ponded up against the retreating ice at the end of the last ice age. In 1855 or 1856, part of the Barrier collapsed, and an enormous landslide swept down the Cheakamus River for some distance. There are remains of many other landslides in the area; if you are sharp-eyed you may spot some.

The Meager volcanic complex last erupted about 2400 years ago. You can see signs of this recent volcanic activity in a canyon on the Lillooet River, and you can see how the river has cut down through deposits of pumice and ash (see photo). The Meager Creek hotsprings nearby suggest that there is still magma beneath the surface.

The Coast Mountains are just coming out of the ice age. The many U-

The Lillooet River has cut through this 80-m wall of ash near Meager Creek in the last 2400 years.

and V-shaped and hanging valleys hint at how recent the retreat of the ice was. But the most obvious indications of present glaciation are the huge ice sheets that can been seen from many places along the roads. Numerous trails give access to the edges of the glaciers and icefields and provide a close-up look at these features.

The geography of the Whistler region, whether it be physical, social, economic, or historical, is shaped by the mountains. As you cross the Coast Mountains from west to east there are three separate geographic regions. The westernmost abuts the coastline and is characterized by steep, heavily forested terrain that rises to about 2000 m. It is penetrated by fjords to a substantial distance inland; Howe Sound is a good example of a fjord. Beyond the heads of the inlets is the backbone of the Coast Mountains. The mountains form a barrier that towers 1000 m or more above the coastal peaks. It is this barrier that traps the moisture-laden storms that try to cross it. The precipitation that is dumped here creates rain forests at the lower levels and glaciers and icefields, some of the largest in the temperate world, at higher elevations. The easternmost region lies on the interior side of the mountains where they fade into the interior plateaus. Here the mountains are between 2500 and 3000 m high but are nowhere near as rugged as on the coast, and the valley bottoms are of a friendlier nature. Here on the lee side of the mountains the vegetation is thinner, glaciation lighter, and the alpine meadows more extensive.

Although the Coast Mountains have the reputation for being wet throughout the year, you have to remember that the mountains create a great diversity of climates. The coastal side of the mountains has warm, wet winters and cool, drier summers. Further inland there is less precipitation and a greater contrast between summer and winter temperatures. For these reasons I suggest that you plan an inland trip if it is too wet and move waterward if the temperature is too extreme.

The mountains have the effect of preventing weather systems from moving on, so once a storm has moved in it tends to take longer to clear up than it does in Vancouver or the interior. Statistically, May, late July and September have the best weather, but there are great variations from year to year. The mountains also create a host of microclimates that are masked by the macroclimates but which are very important ecologically. When you go on a trip go prepared to find extreme differences along the trail as you wander in and out of various microclimates. There are places where it is said, "If you don't like the weather wait fifteen minutes and it will change." The Coast Mountains version of this is "move a kilometre and it will be different."

Fauna and Flora

For all the human intrusion that has occurred, the area surrounding Whistler and Pemberton still contains vast areas of true wilderness. This wilderness continues to support all the wildlife of yesteryear but not necessarily in the same numbers. The wildlife here is true *wild*life and makes itself scarce when humans are around. Moose, grizzly and cougars have all been sighted in recent years from the major roads in the Pemberton Valley. If a nature guide indicates an animal exists within this area, then it certainly does, but don't count on seeing it unless you have a lot of patience or luck. As with the animals, all the birds reckoned to be within this area can be spotted if one takes the time. Bald eagles are present all year but are most common in the fall and winter. The usual selection of B.C. fish are found here with rainbow trout, Dolly Varden and salmon being the most common.

The plant communities of this area are dominated, at least visually, by the coniferous trees but they are far from the only form of plant life in the region. A proper set of field guides is required to identify many of the plants that grow here.

The great changes in climate in this region, both across the Coast

Wildlife can be found anywhere

Mountains and vertically within the mountains, means that within the space of a short distance there are great changes in the floral make-up. A drive from Squamish to Lillooet takes you from an area dominated by western hemlock to one dominated by Ponderosa pine while going up through an area where alpine fir is prevalent. A walk along the bottom of a hillside will take you from a climax forest of red cedar to a logged area where fireweed and alder are common and then to a stream bed where devil's club will be the most common plant.

Access

Approach routes in the Whistler area are constantly and rapidly changing. Highway 99 is being improved, and new logging roads are built as old ones fall into disrepair. Trails are being upgraded and rerouted constantly. These changes may result in slightly different mileages than those given in this book. Some access routes and methods may be restricted. For example, mechanical methods of transport such as mountain bikes and snowmobiles are prohibited in the parks. Travel on active logging roads is commonly restricted to evenings and weekends, and all off-road travel may be prohibited during periods of high fire hazard. Any restrictions are usually prominently posted on the roads and in stores, or ask at the B.C. Forest Service (BCFS) office.

Even if the roads change slightly you should be able to find the start of most of the trips. However, if you are planning on using something other than hiking boots or skis inside Garibaldi Park, you should heed the restrictions posted at trailheads.

Main Access Roads

It is from these roads that the various trips begin. All distances were measured using the "Beast." Your mileages might be slightly different.

- **Highway 99:** This is the paved highway from Vancouver to Pemberton. All distances are measured from Whistler Village. South-bound distances are towards Squamish and north-bound distances are towards Pemberton.

- **D'Arcy road:** From the northern end of Highway 99, this is the road that branches right. It is paved all the way through Mount Currie to Devine and D'Arcy, a distance of 44.5 km. An extremely rough 4x4 road branches off as you enter D'Arcy and goes to Seton Portage.

- **Duffey Lake road:** A well-marked, popular route from Pemberton to Lillooet. From the church in Mount Currie it is 88.1 km to the Shantyman Coffee Shop in Lillooet. The road runs along the Birkenhead River to Lillooet Lake before starting steeply uphill at the 10 km mark. The pavement climbs steeply to the 24 km mark before levelling off. The road is paved except for the first 10 km out of Mount Currie and is kept open in the winter unless there is high avalanche hazard.

- **East Lillooet River road:** This gravel road starts at the 10 km mark on the Duffey Lake road and runs down the east side of the Lillooet River to the Spring Creek logging camp at the north end of Harrison Lake. The entire road can be travelled by most cars. The ends of the road are heavily travelled by logging trucks and are thus in good condition. However the middle section is relatively narrow, winding and rough, requiring careful driving. From the Spring Creek logging camp, a 4x4 road continues south to the Fraser Valley.

- **West Lillooet River road:** This gravel road is reached by going down the east Lillooet River road to kilometre 29 where a bridge crosses the river. On the west side, one road goes about 10 km upriver and along Lillooet Lake before ending. The main road turns left after crossing the bridge and runs downstream to rejoin the east Lillooet River road.

- **Upper Lillooet River road:** This road runs left from the fork at the northern end of Highway 99 up the Lillooet River. One kilometre up the road is the village of Pemberton. At kilometre 23.6, the road forks, with one continuing up the southwest side of the river (30+ km) while the right fork crosses over to the northeast side of the river and continues up to Meager Creek hotsprings. The road is paved to where it crosses the Lillooet.

- **Hurley River road:** This is a logging road that starts at the 32.3 km mark of the upper Lillooet road and goes to Gold Bridge, where it connects with the Gold Bridge road.

- **Gold Bridge road:** The good gravel highway that runs between Lillooet and Gold Bridge. It provides access to roads that lead to Seton Portage, Shalalth and Bralorne.

In the following mileage charts, use the left column and read up if you are travelling from the bottom destination towards the top. Use the right column and read down if you are going the other way. For example, if you are travelling along Highway 99, Daisy Lake is 24.0 km from Whistler and 32.6 km from Squamish. In general, the end of the road closest to Whistler is at the bottom of the log.

Highway 99 south of Whistler

Distances are measured between the traffic lights in Squamish and the lights at Whistler Village.

56.6 —	0.0 km	**Squamish**
52.8 —	3.8 km	Diamond Head turnoff
52.2 —	4.4 km	Garibaldi Highlands
47.0 —	9.6 km	Alice Lake turnoff
42.6 —	14.0 km	Brohm Lake
39.0 —	17.6 km	Tantalus viewpoint 2
30.6 —	26.0 km	Tantalus viewpoint
24.6 —	32.0 km	Black Tusk turnoff
24.0 —	32.6 km	Daisy Lake
21.9 —	34.7 km	Black Tusk village (south)
20.9 —	35.7 km	Black Tusk village (north)
17.8 —	38.8 km	BCFS Brandywine Falls
12.9 —	43.7 km	Calcheak Campsite
12.4 —	44.2 km	Callaghan Lake road
12.1 —	44.5 km	basalt columns
8.0 —	48.6 km	BCR crossing
7.4 —	49.2 km	Cheakamus Lake turnoff
3.9 — —	52.7 km	Whistler Creek (Gondola)
0.0 —	56.6 km	**Whistler Village**

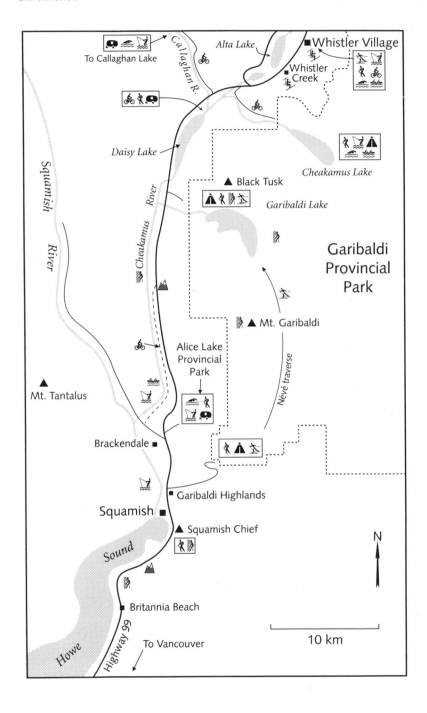

Highway 99 north of Whistler

Distances are measured between the traffic lights in Whistler Village and the T-junction at the north end of Highway 99 near Pemberton.

31.9 —	0.0 km	T-junction – **Pemberton** west, D'Arcy east
30.7 —	1.2 km	One Mile Lake
28.9 —	3.0 km	Nairn Falls Provincial Park
24.3 —	7.6 km	Rutherford Creek road
24.1 —	7.8 km	Rutherford Creek bridge
16.6 —	15.3 km	Soo River bridge
16.4 —	15.5 km	Soo River road
12.1 —	19.8 km	Wedgemount parking area
9.2 —	22.7 km	Cougar Mountain
7.6 —	24.3 km	Emerald Estates (north)
6.9 —	25.0 km	Emerald Estates (south)
3.9 —	28.0 km	Alpine Meadows
3.3 —	28.6 km	River of Golden Dreams
3.0 —	28.9 km	Green Lake turnoff
0.0 —	31.9 km	**Whistler Village**

Duffey Lake road

Distances are between the church in Mount Currie and the Shantyman Restaurant in Lillooet.

88.1 —	0.0 km	**Lillooet** – Shantyman Restaurant
84.5 —	3.6 km	Seton Lake campsite (B.C. Hydro)
83.7 —	4.4 km	Seton Lake boat launch
81.0 —	7.1 km	pavement begins/ends
76.3 —	11.8 km	Cayoosh Creek crossing
69.9 —	18.2 km	BCFS Cinnamon campsite
66.4 —	21.7 km	BCFS Cottonwood campsite
59.4 —	28.7 km	BCFS Gott Creek campsite
57.9 —	30.3 km	BCFS Rogers Creek campsite
57.4 —	30.7 km	BCFS Second Crossing campsite
43.1 —	45.0 km	Blowdown Creek turnoff
41.6 —	46.5 km	BCFS Duffey Lake campsite
41.1 —	47.0 km	Duffey Lake boat launch
34.8 —	53.3 km	Van Horlick Creek turnoff
23.6 —	64.5 km	Cerise Creek turnoff
22.6 —	65.5 km	BCFS Joffre Lakes campsite
10.0 —	78.1 km	Lillooet Lake east side road turnoff
5.6 —	82.5 km	Xit'olacw turnoff
0.0 —	88.1 km	**Mount Currie** church and D'Arcy road

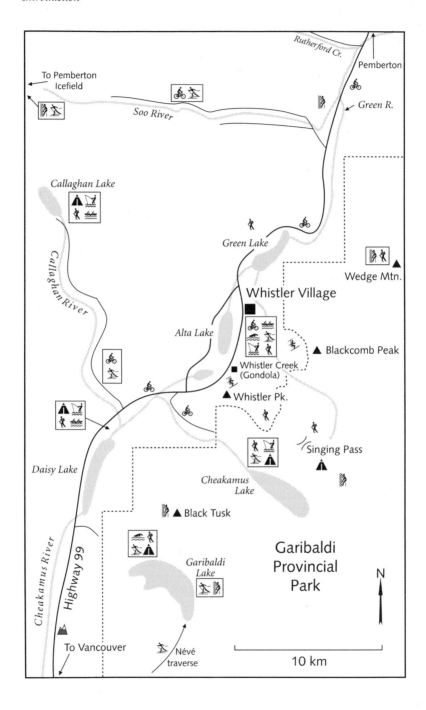

To Pemberton Icefield

Rutherford Cr.

Pemberton

Green R.

Soo River

Callaghan Lake

Callaghan River

Green Lake

Wedge Mtn.

Whistler Village

Alta Lake

Blackcomb Peak

Whistler Creek (Gondola)

Whistler Pk.

Singing Pass

Daisy Lake

Cheakamus Lake

Black Tusk

Cheakamus River

Highway 99

Garibaldi Lake

Garibaldi Provincial Park

N

To Vancouver

Névé traverse

10 km

D'Arcy road

Distances are measured between the T-junction at the northern terminus of Highway 99 and D'Arcy at the west end of Anderson Lake. The road is the one to the right.

44.5 —	0.0 km	D'Arcy and Anderson Lake
39.5 —	5.5 km	turnoff – south to Devine, north to Birkenhead Lake Provincial Park
28.0 —	16.5 km	Birken
13.0 —	31.5 km	Birkenhead River bridge
11.1 —	33.4 km	BCFS Owl Creek campsite
7.2 —	37.3 km	BCR tracks
6.6 —	37.9 km	Mount Currie church – Duffey Lake road turnoff
2.1 —	42.4 km	Lillooet River bridge
1.8 —	42.7 km	Pemberton Airport turnoff
0.0 —	44.5 km	north end of Highway 99

Lillooet River east side road

Distances are between the turnoff at the 10 km mark on the Duffey Lake road and the Spring Creek logging camp at the north end of Harrison Lake.

85.6 —	0.0 km	**Spring Creek logging camp**
80.6 —	5.0 km	Sloquet Creek bridge
79.0 — —	6.6 km	right angle bend
75.5 —	10.1 km	**junction with west side road** (see below)
74.5 —	11.1 km	Harrison – Lillooet trail parking
71.2 —	14.4 km	Port Douglas turnoff (to east)
55.1 —	30.5 km	Harrison – Lillooet trail parking
54.5 —	31.1 km	Gowan Creek bridge
49.6 —	36.0 km	Skookumchuck village
46.1 —	39.5 km	Skookumchuck hotsprings (power pole 68.2)
43.5 —	42.1 km	Rogers Creek logging road
43.0 —	43.6 km	Rogers Creek bridge
38.4 —	47.2 km	Squamaquam hill
33.3 —	52.3 km	Harrison – Lillooet trail parking
29.0 —	47.6 km	**turnoff to west side road** (see below)
23.9 —	61.7 km	south end of Lillooet Lake
16.6 —	69.0 km	BCFS Driftwood Bay campsite
15.4 —	70.2 km	Lizzie Creek road
14.8 —	70.8 km	BCFS Lizzie Bay campsite
9.7 —	75.9 km	BCFS Twin One Bay campsite
9.0 —	76.6 km	Twin One logging road turnoff
6.5 —	79.1 km	BCFS Strawberry Point campsite
0.0 —	85.6 km	**Duffey Lake road**

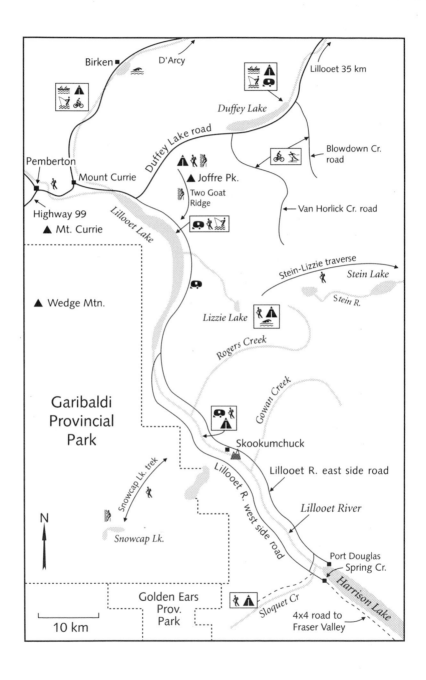

Birken ■   D'Arcy

Lillooet 35 km

Duffey Lake

Duffey Lake road

Blowdown Cr.
road

Pemberton

Mount Currie

▲ Joffre Pk.

Two Goat
Ridge

◄— Van Horlick Cr. road

Highway 99
▲ Mt. Currie

Lillooet Lake

Stein-Lizzie traverse

Stein Lake

▲ Wedge Mtn.

Stein R.

Lizzie Lake

Rogers Creek

Gowan Creek

Garibaldi
Provincial
Park

Skookumchuck

Snowcap Lk. trek

Lillooet R. east side road

Lillooet R. west side road

Lillooet River

N

Snowcap Lk.

Port Douglas
Spring Cr.

Harrison Lake

Golden Ears
Prov.
Park

Sloquet Cr

4x4 road to
Fraser Valley

10 km

Lillooet River west side road

46.3 —	10.1 km	junction with east side road
24.3 —	32.1 km	logging road
23.6 —	32.8 km	logging road
21.7 —	34.7 km	logging road
9.0 —	47.4 km	mining camp
0.5 —	55.9 km	Tenas Lake bridge
0.0 —	56.5 km	junction with east side road

Upper Lillooet River road

Distances are between the northern terminus of Highway 99 and Meager Creek hotsprings.

68.3 —	0.0 km	**Meager Creek hotsprings** parking lot
68.0 —	0.3 km	gate
66.9 —	1.4 km	Meager Creek bridge
66.0 —	2.3 km	logging road
60.2 —	8.1 km	Lillooet River headwaters straight ahead
32.3 —	37.2 km	Hurley road
26.4 —	41.9 km	outdoor school
25.1 —	43.2 km	Lillooet River bridge
23.6 —	44.7 km	fork; turn right
7.3 —	61.0 km	Ryan River
2.7 —	65.6 km	intersection; turn left
2.5 —	65.8 km	Pemberton High School
1.0 —	67.3 km	ScotiaBank; turn right
0.9 —	67.4 km	**Pemberton**
0.0 —	68.3 km	north end of Highway 99

Hurley River road

Distances are between the upper Lillooet road and the Bailey bridge just outside Gold Bridge.

49.0 —	0.0 km	**Gold Bridge** Bailey bridge
48.8 —	0.2 km	Gun Lake road
45.3 —	3.7 km	logging road
43.3 —	5.7 km	BCFS Gwyneth Lake campsite
32.7 —	16.3 km	BCFS Hurley River campsite; turn to Bralorne
14.5 —	34.5 km	Railroad Pass
10.4 —	38.6 km	fork; go right
0.0 —	49.0 km	**upper Lillooet River road**

Gold Bridge road

Distances are between the Bailey bridge just outside Gold Bridge and the Shantyman Restaurant in Lillooet.

104.9	—	0.0 km	**Lillooet** – Shantyman Restaurant
104.4	—	0.5 km	Bridge of 23 Camels turnoff
103.7	—	1.2 km	BCR tracks
102.7	—	2.2 km	Government building
101.7	—	3.2 km	Main Street straight ahead
95.0	—	9.9 km	bridge
71.2	—	33.7 km	logging road
70.2	—	34.7 km	Yalakom River
65.7	—	39.2 km	overhanging rock
55.0	—	49.9 km	dam and turnoff to Seton Portage
34.8	—	70.1 km	logging road
11.3	—	93.6 km	**Tyax Mountain Lake Resort turnoff** (see below)
6.0	—	98.9 km	**Gun Lake turnoff** (see below)
0.2	—	104.7 km	**Gold Bridge** and Bralorne turnoff
0.0	—	104.9 km	logging road; bear left

Gun Lake road

22.1	—	0.0 km	Jewel Creek bridge
18.0	—	4.1 km	logging road
15.4	—	6.7 km	logging road
14.5	—	7.6 km	airport road straight ahead; turn left
12.3	—	9.8 km	BCFS Gun Lake south campsite
7.1	—	15.0 km	BCFS Gun Lake campsite
6.5	—	15.6 km	gravel road
6.2	—	15.9 km	Lajoie Lake
1.2	—	20.9 km	Gun Lake turn (double back)
0.0	—	22.1 km	Gold Bridge and Hurley River roads

Tyax Mountain Lake Resort branch

8.4	—	0.0 km	Tyax Mountain Lake Resort
7.9	—	0.5 km	BCFS Tyaughton Lake campsite
3.4	—	5.0 km	gravel road
0.0	—	8.4 km	Gold Bridge road

Accommodation and Services

Towns

- **Squamish:** Largest town in the area, on Highway 99 about halfway between Vancouver and Whistler. The area population is 12 000+. A complete range of services is available but the selection of speciality shops is limited. The Chamber of Commerce (892-9244) can provide more information.

- **Garibaldi Highlands:** Located 5 km north of Squamish at the traffic lights on Highway 99. There is a shopping mall beside the highway. Shares services with Squamish and Brackendale.

- **Brackendale:** Situated 8 km north of Squamish west of Highway 99. Shares services with Squamish and Garibaldi Highlands. There is a small mall in the town. Squamish Airport is just north of the town.

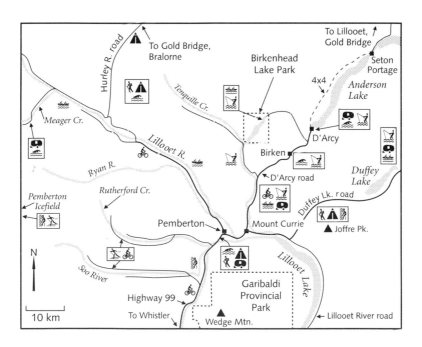

- **Whistler:** Popular year round resort 120 km north of Vancouver on Highway 99. A complete range of tourist and community services and shops is available. Ski equipment, bike, and canoe rentals are available. Helicopter and float plane charter services. Stores are open seven days a week. You can book many activities through the Whistler Activities and Information Centre at 932-2394. The Chamber of Commerce (932-5528) can provide more information.

- **Pemberton:** This small town is the main service centre for the Pemberton Valley. It has the standard small town set of services and an airport with paved runway. Helicopter service located 7 km north of town.

- **Mount Currie:** The Mount Currie Indian Reserve has a population of about 850 and is located 6.6 km east of Pemberton. The Spirit Circle, which serves native foods and sells native crafts, is worth visiting.

- **Xit'olacw:** Reached by turning off the Duffey Lake road 5.6 km down from the church in Mount Currie. There is a small store 4 km off the Duffey Lake road.

- **Skookumchuck:** Located 4.1 km south of Skookumchuck hotsprings, with a population of about 100. The famous "Mall-in-the-Hall" has a very small stock of essential food supplies. Gas may be available.

- **Port Douglas:** A mining camp and Indian village at the north end of Harrison Lake on the east corner. No services or facilities.

- **Spring Creek:** A logging camp at the north end of Harrison Lake on the west side. No services or facilities.

- **Lillooet:** On the west side of the Fraser River on Highway 12, about 240 km from Vancouver and 180 km west of Kamloops. A complete but limited range of services, helicopter charter service, and an airport are available. Most stores open six days a week from 9:00 a.m. to 6:00 p.m.

- **Gold Bridge:** Small village on the Hurley road about halfway between Pemberton and Lillooet. Very limited range of services and a gas station, open six days a week from 9:00 a.m. to 5:30 p.m. There are two hotels in the town and several resorts in the surrounding area.

- **Bralorne:** Located 11 km south of Gold Bridge. Very few services.

- **Birken:** Located beside Gates Lake on the D'Arcy road, 9.9 km from Mount Currie. Restaurant, gas, cabins and camping available.

- **D'Arcy:** Situated at the end of Anderson Lake, 37.7 km from Mount Currie. Small general store, gas and cottages available. Camping spots on lake.

Commercial Accommodation and Campsites

Whistler, Squamish, and Lillooet have a wide variety of hotels and motels. Pemberton, Mount Currie, Gold Bridge and D'Arcy each have at least one hotel or motel. The Whistler Resort Association has a central reservation number (932-4222) to book any hotel, condo, or bed-and-breakfast in Whistler. Commercial campsites are available in spring, summer and fall in Whistler, D'Arcy, Mount Currie, and Lillooet.

Provincial Parks

The following parks have provisions for camping. The supervised campgrounds have a small overnight fee and stays are limited to 14 days.

- **Alice Lake:** 95 campsites, picnic tables, fishing, swimming, sani-station.
- **Garibaldi:** Wilderness park, wilderness camping and picnicking. In the Garibaldi Lake area, camping is permitted in designated areas only.
- **Nairn Falls:** 86 campsites, sani-station, and fishing.
- **Birkenhead Lake:** 85 campsites, picnicking, swimming, fishing, boat launch and sani-station.

B.C. Forest Service Campsites

These sites are rustic and usually small with room for less than 10 vehicles and/or tents. They do not offer sophisticated amenities such as power hookups and piped water, but do include outhouses, fire rings and picnic tables. Some have boat launches and floats.

The sites are designated as small (under 10 vehicles), medium (11 to 20), and large (over 20). The sites are user maintained, meaning that you have to pack out your own garbage. If there are litter barrels they are to be used for non-food items. Firewood is not provided at these sites. Either bring your own or collect dead wood in the area. Try collecting your firewood a few kilometres down the road from the campsite to ease the pressure on the immediate area. Please keep fires small. Some of these sites are heavily used, particularly on weekends. Noise and party animals are often a problem.

The B.C. Forest Service offices in Squamish and Lillooet provide free, updated Forest Service recreation maps that show the locations of the campsites and important access routes.

Highway 99

- **Calcheak confluence:** Located south of Whistler just off Highway 99. There are three medium sized camping areas in the forest.

- **Callaghan Lake:** A medium sized site on the lake up the Callaghan River road turnoff. Usually not open until July because of snow.

Suspension bridge at the Calcheak campsite

D'Arcy road

- **Mosquito Lake:** A small open site north of Mount Currie off the D'Arcy road, with the final approach along a rutted track.

- **Owl Creek:** A large semi-open area divided into two sites. This spot is suitable for large groups.

- **Spetch Creek:** A medium sized, wooded site beside a creek.

- **Blackwater Lake:** A medium sized site on the road to Birkenhead Lake Provincial Park. There is a small float at the water's edge.

Lillooet River and Lake roads

- **Strawberry Point:** A medium sized site on the lake. A five minute walk from parking lot to camping spots on the sandy beach.

- **Twin One Creek:** A medium sized site that is mostly open. Boats can be launched.

- **Lizzie Bay:** A large site on Lillooet Lake. Access road to sites is narrow, so long vehicles are not recommended.

- **Driftwood Bay:** A medium sized site on Lillooet Lake.

- **Lizzie Lake:** A small site on Lizzie Lake five minutes from the car. Four-wheel drive recommended for access.

- **Meager Creek:** A large site with treed overnight camping area. Five minutes walk to the hotsprings.

Duffey Lake road

- **Joffre Alpine:** Small open site at the Joffre Alpine Recreational Area.

- **Duffey Lake:** A medium sized, semi-open site with a boat launch 400 m to the west.

- **Cayoosh Creek:** A very small site best for picnicking.

- **Rogers Creek:** A large semi-open site with good fishing.

- **Gott Creek:** A medium sized open site.

- **Cottonwood:** A small treed site.

- **Cinnamon:** A small semi-open site.

- **Seton Lake:** A medium sized site reached by 4-wheel drive from kilo-metre 20 (west of Lillooet along the Duffey Lake road) or by boat. Narrow beach and fishing.

Gold Bridge and Hurley River roads

These sites are listed in the order they are encountered driving from east to west (Lillooet to Pemberton). Many are well off the main roads.

- **Mission Dam:** A medium sized site with fishing.

- **Carpenter Lake:** A small site with a boat launch.

- **Jones Creek:** A medium sized site with fishing.

- **Carol Lake:** A large open site with fishing and trails to other fishing lakes.

- **Marshall Creek:** A small treed site.

- **Marshall Lake north:** A medium sized, semi-open site. Good access for pickups.

- **Liza Creek:** A small site with good fishing access to Liza Lake.

- **Tyax junction:** A small site with a limited boat launch.

- **Mowson Pond:** A medium sized, semi-open site with good fishing.

- **Pearson Pond:** Small site with good summer and winter fishing.

- **Gun Creek:** A large, semi-open site with fishing.

- **Gun Lake south:** A medium sized site.

- **Lost Lake:** A medium sized, semi-open site with fishing, 5 minutes walk from parking area.

- **Kingdom Lake:** Small treed site with good fishing.

- **Gwyneth Lake:** A medium sized site with good fishing.

- **Hurley River:** A small site between Gold Bridge and Pemberton used as a rest stop.

Wilderness Shelters

These shelters consist of little more than four walls and a roof. They have one room, a table or two, and a nearby outhouse. They were built by individuals and outdoor organizations and are open to the public without charge, on a first-come basis. Because of their small size you should carry a tent during high usage times such as weekends. They are great to hang out and cook meals in during periods of bad weather. Treat them with respect.

- **Wedgemount Lake:** Small shelter that holds 8 people.

- **Diamond Head, Red Heather:** A rest-stop shelter with tables.

- **Diamond Head, Elfin Lakes:** Large (house size) shelter that holds about 40, with indoor outhouses and a wood stove. Small overnight charge.

- **Black Tusk, Battleship Islands:** Several shelters with tables and wood stoves. Popular camping spot in the winter.

- **Sphinx Glacier (Garibaldi Lake):** Small shelter that sleeps 8 people.

- **Lizzie Meadows:** Small log cabin that sleeps 8 people. Table and wood stove.

- **Trigger Lake, Warner Pass:** Medium sized log cabin that sleeps 15 people. Tables and wood stove.

- **Singing Pass, Russet Lake:** Small shelter that sleeps 8 people.

Lowland Walks

These walks can be done by just about anyone in any weather, but you'll enjoy them most if the sun is shining. They are short with little elevation gain, yet lead to the most exquisite places. The walks vary in length from a few hundred metres to a few level kilometres along good, easy to follow trails. As for equipment, a pair of feet, preferably with a good pair of footwear on them (reasonably water-proof with a non-slip sole), a camera, and a pack with munchies will do.

Because of their short length, these walks are great for a lazy afternoon. Take your time, perhaps all day if you are going to relax at the destination point.

Now pick a walk and go for a walk.

Lost Lake

Swimming... Walking... Picnicking... Mountain biking...
Cross-country skiing

Located beside Whistler Village, the trails around Lost Lake offer a variety of activities year round and let you get away from the hustle and bustle of the village.

Trail length: 7 km maximum
Hiking time: 2 hours or less

Location: Beside Whistler Village
　　　　20 minute walk

Distance from Whistler Village: 2 km

Approach instructions:
(1) The Lost Lake parking lot is small and usually full. Park in Whistler Village and follow the path past the Chateau Whistler to the golf course parking area. During the busy summer months a shuttle bus runs from here to the lake.
(2) From Whistler Village head across the day-skier parking lots to a noticeboard with a map of the trails on it.

 Hiking: Kilometres of well maintained trails.

 Mountain biking: Great trails on undulating terrain for the beginner.

 Swimming: A rarity – a warm lake that is well protected from wind, and several sandy beaches with floats.

 Picnic sites: A limited number of tables and barbeques, but lots of nice grass.

Cross-country skiing: Groomed trails and warming hut.

 Canoeing: Flat water canoeing on a calm lake. Great for the first timer.

From the parking lot at Lost Lake, head down to the lake where a developed beach area provides a place for a picnic and swim. The obvious trail takes you counterclockwise around the lake. The route stays close to the shore until you get to the far corner where it cuts a little further inland. As it winds around the lake, the trail goes up and down a series of hills that tire you then relax you. On the far side of the lake, follow the trail along Blackcomb Creek to a bridge, where the trail from Whistler Village comes in. Turn left here and cross another bridge to return to the picnic tables.

This picturesque lake in the mountains has all the qualities needed to make this a lovely place for swimming on a hot day. Because it is fed by snowmelt rather than glaciers, the water starts life a little warmer. The water runs a considerable distance (relatively speaking) over warm ground before reaching the lake, making it warmer still. The turnover of water in the lake is high enough to cleanse the water and get rid of stagnant odours, yet slow enough that the water warms up under the rays of the summer sun. Being in a basin, the lake is protected from cooling by the wind, which makes emerging from the water more pleasant for scantily-clad swimmers.

At the end opposite to the beach, you can see changes in the types of trees. It is tempting to think that large numbers of red cedar and wild cherry grow here because they prefer the marshier conditions. But it isn't; rather it is that they compete better under these conditions. It might seem like nitpicking but it's not. What's the difference? To use an analogy, a person two metres tall makes a better basketball player than a person a metre and half, because height is advantageous in basketball. If the shorter person is better coordinated and the two of them play in a sport where coordination is critical, then the shorter one competes more successfully. In the case of marshy conditions, where the soil is more acidic and less oxygen is available for the roots, the cedars and cherries compete better. So, like the shorter person who enjoys basketball but takes up a different competitive sport to be more successful, the cedar and cherry live in the marsh. Take away the tall people and the short person plays basketball. Take away hemlocks and Douglas firs, and the cedars and cherries will thrive in the relatively dry environment by the beach.

The Lost Lake trails are popular all year round, especially in the summer with bikers and walkers and in the winter with cross-country skiers. They should not be forgotten in the early fall when the quietness of the season gives them their greatest beauty.

Alpine Blackcomb

*Alpine walks ... Access on chairlift ... Views of Whistler ...
Mountain lake ... Mountain bike riding ... Meadows ... In
Whistler Village*

A chairlift ride to the alpine meadows at the top of Blackcomb with a magnificent view of Whistler Village, the Whistler valley, the backcountry of Garibaldi Park and the Pemberton Icefield.

Various trails lead to alpine meadows and tarns and up the mountains. All provide good walks on stony terrain. After mountain biking on these trails you can ride to the Village.

Trail length: 4 km
Hiking time: 3–4 hours

Location: At the top of the Blackcomb ski lifts in Whistler
10 minute walk from Whistler Village

Walking time from Whistler Village: 10 minutes

Approach instructions: Park in the day-skier lot adjacent to Whistler Village and follow the path across a lovely timber-covered bridge to the base of Blackcomb.

Hiking: A series of easy walks with varying elevation gains. A brochure is available at the lift.

Mountain biking: A number of trails are open to mountain bikers. Descent routes to the valley exist. Check available brochure. You can take your bike up on the chairlift.

Skiing: Summer alpine skiing on the glacier (June 15–Aug. 1).

Swimming: Refreshingly nippy summer swimming in Blackcomb Lake.

There are many ways to reach the alpine regions: you can hike up, cheap but physically demanding; or helicopter up, easy but financially demanding. Between these two extremes is the more common summertime method of taking a chairlift up. It is easy on both pocketbook and body yet achieves the same result.

Buy a ticket at the bottom of Blackcomb and catch the Wizard chair up. Halfway up the mountain you transfer to a second lift which takes you to the Rendezvous Restaurant at the 1860 m level.

Here you can sit and admire the views of Whistler Village at your feet and the Pemberton Icefield on the horizon to the west. A map by the restaurant's entrance and brochures inside show all the trails available to you and the sights along them. The trails for the most part are short and, although not flat, involve only gentle climbs. In general, they conform to the ski runs and are easy to follow, although somewhat rocky.

You might consider walking the Southside Trail to Blackcomb Lake. To reach it, take the shuttle bus from the Rendezvous to the base of the Seventh Heaven Express. From here, a round-trip walk of 4 km treats you to an expanse of alpine flowers (at their best in late July) and a beautiful lake. There are fine views across to Whistler and the glaciers and mountains beyond. After your hike, take the Seventh Heaven chair to the top. Here you are on the edge of a mountain ridge looking down on the Horstman Glacier where people ski throughout the summer. High above the timberline and alpine meadows in the land of rock and ice, sit and admire the views in all directions. When you have finished enjoying the view, if you ever do, you can either hike down to the restaurant or descend on the chair back to the bus.

Just as it is necessary to leave the front seat of the automobile to fully appreciate a great museum or cathedral, so it is necessary to walk a bit (preferably a great deal) to gain a true appreciation of these living museums of nature.

Brian Patton
Canadian Rockies Trail Guide

Cougar Mountain

Giant cedars and Douglas firs . . . Easy walk . . . Great mountain biking . . . Cross-country skiing . . . Swimming . . . Within Whistler municipality

Douglas firs and cedar up to 12 m around that can be reached at any time of the year. Drive up to the trailhead on a gravel road that gets rougher as it goes up, or walk from Highway 99.

This is a straightforward mountain bike ride from Whistler Village with a stiff climb on the gravel road. A short trail near the end of the gravel road leads to a lake.

Trail length: 12 km return from pavement
    4 km return from end of gravel road
Elevation change: 400 m from pavement
    150 m from end of gravel road
Walking time: 4 hours round trip from pavement
    1½ hours round trip from end of gravel road

Location: North end of Whistler Municipality
    10 minutes from Whistler Village

Driving distance from Whistler Village: 9.2 km

Driving instructions: From Whistler Village, drive 9.2 km north on Highway 99 to a gravel road that takes off to the left. Drive up the road until it gets too rough. Go right at all forks. Park well off the road.

 Hiking: Easy walking but with a couple of steep inclines.

 Mountain biking: Good riding but requires some puffing. A great trip for intermediate riders.

 Cross-country skiing: A nice safe ski for intermediate level skiers who have never ventured off tracks.

Wheelchairs: From the end of the gravel road it is a reasonable trip over rugged ground. The initial climb from the gravel into the woods is steep.

Swimming: Good swimming in Showh Lake at the end of the gravel road.

Cougar Mountain is possibly the best all-everything, all-season trip in the Whistler valley. The main goal is a grove of cedars that may be a thousand years old and Douglas firs that are 650 years old. Many of these trees are more than 8 m in circumference. The nicest thing about this grove is that it can be reached by anyone in the summer and is accessible to most people throughout the year.

To reach the area, drive 9.2 km north on Highway 99 from Whistler Village to the north end of Green Lake, where a logging road takes off to the left. You can either park just off the pavement or drive up the road. Although it is possible to drive up to Showh Lake, the road is quite rough and you may want to stop before you reach the lake. If you do, park well off the road.

As you go up the road take the right forks until you reach a small bowl where the road peters out and the trail begins. The climb into mature timber is short and steep, but once in the timber the trail flattens out as it rolls around a sidehill and into the grove. In the grove the trail makes a kilometre-long loop among the trees.

Once in the grove stand for a minute as you might in a cathedral, because that is what you are in: a cathedral of cedars. As you stroll around these monoliths consider that these trees were fully grown before Columbus reached America. In fact, the Douglas firs were seedlings about the time of Richard the Lion-Hearted of England and the cedars started to grow about the time of William the Conqueror.

Two points of biological interest to note as you wander among the trees. Because both Douglas fir and cedar are shade-intolerant species – that is, they cannot grow in the shade – they are not considered to be the climax forest species. A climax species is one that can succeed itself. In this area hemlock is the climax species because the seedling can grow in its parents' shade. This trait is clearly shown by the lack of low branches on both cedar and fir where the light levels are low. The second interesting point is that many of these trees are either hollow or rotten inside because of their great age and so are not the good commercial timber

Cougar Mountain cedars

they seem to be. In fact the loggers often avoid old groves for this very reason.

When you get back to the logging road you might want to take time to go for a swim in Showh Lake. Watch for the short trail to the lake that leaves the road where it swings away from the lake.

This trip makes for a very pleasant afternoon mountain bike ride from the Village. It is an ideal trip for the beginning mountain-biker who is looking for a moderate challenge. In the winter the trip makes a nice backcountry ski trip for the beginning skier, for the road to Showh Lake rises gently and is easy to follow. There is very little avalanche danger along the route.

Cheakamus Lake

Wilderness lake . . . Easy short hike . . . Easy mountain biking . . .
Cross-country skiing . . . Wilderness camping and picnicking
sites . . . Only 16 km from Whistler Village

An almost flat trail winds through tall trees to a spectacular wilderness
mountain lake. An optional flat trail along the lakeshore goes to Singing
Creek. A short side trip leads to a cable car that crosses the Cheakamus.
The trail along Cheakamus Lake offers stunning views of the mountain
peaks and glaciers, and the opportunity to see an old trapper's cabin.

Trail length: 3.2 km to Cheakamus Lake
4.3 km along the lakeshore to Singing Creek
Walking time: 2 hours return to Cheakamus Lake
4 hours return to Singing Creek

Location: At the southern boundary of Whistler Municipality
30 minute drive from Whistler Village

Driving distance from Whistler Village: 16 km
7.4 km highway
8.6 km gravel road

Driving instructions: From Whistler Village, drive 7.4 km south on
Highway 99 to the Cheakamus Lake turnoff. Turn left and drive
0.6 km to fork in the road. Take left fork and drive 8.0 km to
parking lot at the end of the good gravel road.

Hiking: Easy hiking. The cable car crossing leads to the 15-km-
long Helm Creek trail to Black Tusk Meadows and Garibaldi
Lake area.

Mountain biking: Excellent easy biking from the parking lot to
the lake. Biking is prohibited beyond the lake. Pleasant day trip
from Whistler Village.

Cross-country skiing: Excellent easy skiing from the end of the road to the lake. But for most of the winter be prepared to ski from the highway (an additional 8 km), as the gravel road is not plowed.

 Fishing: Limited fishing for rainbow trout.

 Camping: Wilderness camping at near end of the lake and at the end of the trail at Singing Creek.

 Picnic sites: At the near end of the lake.

Cheakamus Lake is one of those trips that lets you stretch your legs and relax at the same time, regardless of the season. In summer you can drive to the end of the road where a short walk over reasonably flat terrain leads to the western end of Cheakamus Lake. Here the views of the green timbered hillsides shooting skyward from this serene lake are something to feast your eyes on, especially when the surrounding mountains are tipped with snow.

As you walk up the trail you will see a marked trail that provides a route to Black Tusk Meadows via Helm Creek. If you have time, wander down to the cable car that crosses the Cheakamus River. The ride across the river and back in the cable car will give you a thrill. The trail on the other side leads 15 km up to the Black Tusk-Garibaldi Lake area (page 73).

From the near (west) end of Cheakamus Lake, the trail wanders along the north shore to Singing Creek. As you get further up the lake the glaciers at the lake's head start to come into view and Mt. Davidson rears its summit rocks in stunning fashion. About two-thirds of the way to Singing Creek you pass an old trapper's cabin, used by trappers in the 1930s to sleep in during the winter. A small wilderness campsite exists at Singing Creek, but for the walker the cabin is the turnaround spot.

Because of the gentle rise and width of the trail, this trip is an ideal introductory cross-country ski trip, even with the additional 8 km you frequently have to ski along the unplowed gravel road.

Mountain bikers can start at the parking lot and ride to the lakeshore, beyond which riding is not permitted. Fitter cyclists will prefer to start their ride in Whistler Village and use the Valley Trail and the gravel road to obtain a nice half day ride over a variety of terrain.

Brandywine Falls and Calcheak

Waterfall 66 metres high . . . Camping . . . Suspension bridge . . .
Easy walking . . . Easy hiking . . . Picnicking

A short walk leads to a spectacular viewpoint and view of Brandywine Falls. Calcheak campsite to the north has camping and a suspension bridge across Callaghan Creek. A lovely woodland trail past several small lakes connects the campsite and Brandywine Provincial Park.

Trail length: 300 m from Brandywine Falls Provincial Park
4 km from Calcheak campsite to Brandywine Falls
Walking time: 10 minutes from Brandywine Falls Park
2–3 hours return from Calcheak campsite

Location: South of Whistler
20 minute drive from Whistler Village

Driving distance from Whistler Village:
17.8 km to Brandywine Falls Provincial Park
12.9 km to Calcheak campsite

Driving instructions:
(1) From Whistler Village drive 17.8 km south to Brandywine Falls Provincial Park.
(2) From Whistler Village drive 12.9 km south and turn left onto a gravel road. Drive 0.5 km along the road to a fork. To the left are two B.C. Forest Service campsites and to the right there is one. It is less than 0.8 km from the fork to any of them. The trail starts in the one to the right.

If you are driving up Highway 99 and want to stretch your legs for a few minutes, stop at Brandywine Falls. If you are camping at the B.C. Forest Service Calcheak campsite and want a quiet walk after a day in Whistler Village, walk to Brandywine Falls. Interested in geology but too lazy to walk far? Try a visit to Brandywine Falls.

From Brandywine Falls Provincial Park beside Highway 99, 17.8 km

Brandywine Falls

south of Whistler, a wide path leads 300 m south to an airy perch overlooking Brandywine Falls.

Although it is fenced in, some people find the viewpoint intimidating, hanging as it does over the drop that was formed by the waterfall as it eroded its way upstream. Several thousand years ago, the falls were a few hundred metres downstream of their present location, and if you were to come back in a few thousand years the waterfall would be under the bridge by the parking lot. The layer of rock at the top of the falls is harder than the rock underneath, consequently it erodes slower than the rock beneath, creating a lip which will break off when it gets too big. And the waterfall will move upstream another few metres.

If you are camped at the Calcheak Forest Service campsites, located 12.9 km south of Whistler and 4.9 km north of Brandywine Falls Park, there is a pleasant trail that connects with the falls. The trail starts in the Calcheak south campsite, located a short distance down the right fork of the logging road after you turn off Highway 99. Begin by crossing Callaghan Creek on a suspension bridge. From the other side the trail rolls over the countryside for 4 km to Brandywine Falls. Although there is no net elevation gain, there are more than enough ups and downs to justify an extra helping at dinner.

Both these trails cross the railroad tracks and wander along their edge so a watchful eye is needed. At all times avoid actually walking on the tracks.

The falls obtained their name from a wager made in 1910. A survey party was locating the railway line when Jack Nelson, the crew boss, bet Bob Mollison, one of the crew, about the height of the falls, with a bottle of brandy against a bottle of wine. Mollison won and Nelson coughed up the brandy to Mollison. Mollison presumably decided not to push his luck and let Nelson name the falls.

Four Lakes Walk

Quiet woodland walk . . . Swimming . . . Camping and picnicking . . . Fishing . . . All-season strolls

A gentle trail, snow-free most of the year, through a number of ecosystems. There are four quiet woodland lakes with magnificent views.

Trail length: 6.5 km loop
Walking time: 2–3 hours

Location: Immediately north of Squamish
45 minutes from Whistler Village
75 minute drive from Vancouver

Driving distance from Whistler Village: 49.0 km

Driving instructions: From Whistler Village drive 47.0 km south on Highway 99 to the Alice Lake turnoff. You can also reach this point by driving north from Squamish for 9.4 km. Turn east off Highway 99 and follow the paved road into the park. Go left at the first fork and park at the sani-station.

Hiking: Easy walks around Alice Lake, and harder strolls to the other lakes.

Swimming: Good safe swimming in Alice Lake and a beach with picnic tables.

Canoeing: Good place for beginners.

Mountain biking: Surrounding logging roads are ideal, especially early or late in the year.

Fishing: The lake is stocked with rainbow trout.

Camping: Alice Lake Provincial Park has 95 campsites and a sani-station.

丼 **Picnic sites:** Picnic tables and changing facilities at the beach.

This picturesque walk can be done at any time of the year because the low elevation and nearby Howe Sound combine to minimize the snow-fall.

From the sani-station the trail leads north to Stump Lake where it forks. If you are short of time, you can circle the lake and return to your car after an easy walk of 1.5 km. If you don't have to get on your way immediately you face a pleasant choice: which view do you want to see – Mt. Garibaldi (left fork) or Mt. Tantalus (right)? It's your choice.

From where the trails that circle Stump Lake rejoin near an islet on the east side of the lake, the trail leads into the forest before emerging above the Cheekye River. As you walk this part of the trail note the microclimate created by the increased dampness due to the nearby river and its effect of the vegetation. This dampness means there is more un-dergrowth, with ferns and mosses predominating.

The trail continues to Fawn Lake, 3 km from your car. Here you can turn right and walk 100 m down to a cleared point overlooking the lake. Reduced moisture in the air and a soil that is well drained by underlying rocks support different vegetation. Salal and Oregon grape, which thrive on dry ground, are common here because they are not as moisture-dependent as ferns and mosses.

Return to the trail and continue straight ahead along an old logging road to Edith Lake, 1 km past Fawn Lake. Go straight ahead at all forks in the morass of roads and don't go uphill.

At Edith Lake plants such as blackberries and alder predominate be-cause of the increased amount of sunlight and the gravelly soil. A short distance along the shore of Edith Lake, take a trail coming in from the right that leads down to Alice Lake.

As you head toward Alice Lake the trail again traverses an area of thick vegetation as it follows a creek. Once at Alice Lake you can walk around it either way and out through the campground and back to your car.

Smoke Bluffs

Rock climbers . . . Canada's rock climbing centre

This circle trail just outside Squamish allows you to see rock climbers in action, close-up.

Trail length: 1–4 km round trip
Walking time: 30 minutes or more

Location: On the east side of Highway 99 directly across from the McDonald's in Squamish
60 minute drive from Whistler Village
60 minute drive from Vancouver

Driving distance from Whistler Village: 60.2 km

Driving instructions: From Whistler Village drive south on Highway 99 for 59.5 km to the lights near the McDonald's in Squamish. Turn left, then immediately left again onto Logger's Lane. Drive 0.7 km to a dirt parking lot on the right side of the road. Because of the limited size of the parking lot, you might consider parking in Squamish and walking to the parking area. This adds 2 km to the round trip.

If you are waiting at the lights in Squamish or sitting in McDonald's on a fine day, it is impossible not to notice the rock climbers on the small cliffs east of Highway 99. These cliffs, called the Smoke Bluffs by rock climbers, receive more climbing traffic than any other area at Squamish. Here beginners learn to climb and experts practise extra-difficult climbing in preparation for the looming walls of the Squamish Chief just south of them. Located adjacent to Highway 99, the trail through the Smoke Bluffs lets the non-climber watch rock climbing close up without having to walk very far.

From the parking lot, follow the trail (or a climber) south underneath the bluffs, ascending slightly as you go. After hiking for about 10 minutes, you reach a housing development. Just beyond the development,

You can't get much closer without actually climbing

after the trail re-enters the woods, a rough trail heads left up into the woods and toward some cliffs. If you have trouble finding the turnoff, ask a climber where the trail to Octopus' Garden is. Once you're on the trail, it is easy to follow. After about 15 minutes and a few flights of stairs, take a set of steps heading downwards; shortly beyond you will see a cliff with a large number of vertical cracks on its right-hand side. This is Octopus' Garden. From here you can either return the way you came or loop around on the slightly fainter trails that emanate from below the cliff.

As you walk along the trail, you will see spur trails that lead off to the cliffs that dot the area. Take some of these and you will be sitting metres – if that – from the climbers and will be able to get an appreciation for their sport. To really understand what's going on, politely ask a climber who is not attached to a rope to explain the intricacies and terminology of the sport. The person who is climbing is obviously the climber. The person who is holding the rope that is attached to the climber is the belayer and is responsible for holding the climber if he falls. The belayer might be at the top of the cliff if he climbed the pitch while trailing a rope behind him. If the belayer is at the bottom of the cliff and the rope goes directly to the climber above, the climber is said to be leading. If the rope runs from the belayer to the top of the cliff and back down to the climber, the climbers are said to be top-roping. If you don't understand, don't worry – the climbers don't bite and most are glad to answer questions.

If you ask the climber only one thing, ask the name of the route they are climbing. The routes often have strange names given to them by the first ascent party. Why? Who knows. Auntie Gravity, Natural Carpet Ride, Flying Circus (lots of falls have been taken here) and Orifice Fish are some of the less bizarre names.

Many of the best rock climbing areas around Squamish are either on or surrounded by private land. Over the years, the climbing community has worked hard to keep these rocks accessible to the general public. The biggest effort to date has been the purchase of the Smoke Bluffs themselves. In the future, the climbing community hopes to improve the parking lots and restrooms, and continue to purchase more cliffs that are on private land, including the Chief itself, which is threatened by quarrying.

If you wish to help, contact the Federation of Mountain Clubs of B.C. at 604-737-3053.

Shannon Falls

One of Canada's highest waterfalls . . . Picnicking . . . Roadside location

Located right beside Highway 99 immediately south of Squamish. A short trail leads from the picnic sites beside the parking lot to the base of the waterfall. The waterfall, 260 m high, is claimed by some to be the fourth highest in Canada.

Trail length: 500 m to base of falls
Walking time: 30 minutes

Location: Just south of Squamish
 60 minute drive from Whistler Village
 60 minute drive from Vancouver

Driving distance from Whistler Village: 59.5 km

Driving instructions: From Whistler Village, drive 59.5 km south on Highway 99, or 3.0 km south from the traffic lights in Squamish. Pull into the parking lot in Shannon Falls Provincial Park.

As you drive along Highway 99 between Vancouver and Whistler it is impossible to miss two features just south of Squamish: the huge rock walls of the Squamish Chief and Shannon Falls. A stop at Shannon Falls offers a break from driving and a view of one of Canada's highest waterfalls. All you have to do is to pull your car into the parking lot at the provincial park beside Highway 99, 3 km south of Squamish.

With a height of 260 m, Shannon Falls may be the fourth highest waterfall in Canada. As with most waterfalls there is some dispute as to the exact height, but there is no doubt that this is one of the highest. Unlike, say, Niagara or Brandywine Falls, Shannon Creek does not plunge over a sharp lip and drop free into a pool at the bottom. Therefore, assigning an exact height is a bit arbitrary. Shannon Falls is definitely not as high as Takakkaw Falls (508 m) in Yoho National Park or

Della Falls (404 m) on Vancouver Island. But you could call it either third or fifth depending how you decide to measure it, as Twin Falls in Yoho National Park (274 m) and Hunlen Falls (253 m) in Tweedsmuir Provincial Park are close enough to make personal judgment a factor.

From the picnic tables in the park, you get a good view of the Squamish valley and Howe Sound. These form one large, natural feature, called a U-shaped valley. Some of the world's most spectacular waterfalls, such as those in California's Yosemite Valley, are in U-shaped valleys. Such valleys were created by massive glaciers flowing down the valley during the last ice age, perhaps ten thousand years ago. The glacier flattened and deepened the valley bottom and steepened the sides, giving it a distinctive "U" shape. When the glacier receded the sea filled in the part below sea level, creating a fjord, a deep steep-sided inlet. British Columbia, like Greenland, Norway, Patagonia and New Zealand, contain some of the world's best examples of fjords.

There's a lot of energy in falling water. For example, a litre of water (a waterbottle full) falling the height of Shannon Falls would produce 0.61 calories of energy, assuming no air resistance and a free fall. If there was a hydro-electric generating plant at the bottom of the falls (thankfully there isn't!), that energy could keep a 100-Watt light bulb burning for 25 seconds. The energy is lost in impact with the ground, which raises the water temperature about 0.5° C over that at the top of the falls.

In a free fall, the water would hit the ground at just over 250 km per hour, having taken a bit over 7 seconds in the trip down.

Nairn Falls

Short walk... Waterfall... Swimming... Picnicking...
Camping

Nairn Falls Provincial Park offers camping and a short walk to a spectacular waterfall that shoots through a narrow gorge as it drops 30 m. Or you can take a 2 km trail to safe swimming at One Mile Lake.

Trail length: 1.8 km to Nairn Falls
1.5 km loop of One Mile Lake
3.0 km connecting trail between Nairn Falls and One Mile Lake
Walking time: 60 minutes return to Nairn Falls
30 minute loop around One Mile Lake
45 minutes one way on connecting trail

Location: Immediately south of Pemberton
30 minutes from Whistler Village

Driving distance from Whistler Village: 28.9 km

Driving instructions: From Whistler Village, drive 28.9 km north on Highway 99 to the turnoff for Nairn Falls campground. The trail starts at the noticeboard in the parking lot. One Mile Lake is on the right side of the highway 1.8 km further north. The connecting trail starts between campsites 85 and 86 in the Nairn Falls campground.

Hiking: Easy hiking to the waterfall from the camping area. The walk around One Mile Lake is flat and suitable for wheelchairs. The connecting trail, which has one steep hill on it, joins the lake and the camping area.

Swimming: Great swimming in One Mile Lake. A small beach and shallow water make it safe for small children.

Mountain biking: A nice rest stop for bikers cycling down to Pemberton from Whistler, or cycling the Pemberton Valley.

 Camping: Nairn Falls Provincial Park has 88 campsites.

 Picnic sites: Limited tables at both Nairn Falls and One Mile Lake.

Turn off Highway 99 at the Nairn Falls Provincial Park just before reaching Pemberton, and you will quickly find yourself at a noticeboard. From the noticeboard, an obvious path leads into the woods and a view of the Green River churning its way seaward 30 m below.

From the viewpoint, turn right and stroll upstream along the undulating thoroughfare for just under 2 km to some granitic slabs from which you can hear a thunderous roar. A bit of careful walking on the slabs and you can gaze at a seemingly jump-acrossable fissure in the rock through which the Green River surges with immense force.

Nairn Falls is in three sections. The upper part is the narrow gap through which the river is forced. Here as the river spills through it with unceasing fury a rising mist creates a rainbow (on a sunny day) that touches both sides of the gap. After descending 10 m the river turns sharply right on its way to another 10-m drop, below which it turns abruptly left and tumbles a final 10 m before flattening out and resuming its normal width. This is a good example of a river cutting through a band of hard rock along intersecting lines of weakness caused by faults or joints. In both the river itself and on the slab upon which you stand you will notice circular shafts descending into the rock. These are potholes, created by the scouring action of stones and gravel on the hard rock at some time in the past.

After you return from the falls you can drive north 2 km to One Mile Lake, or if you are feeling energetic you can hike there. The trail starts between campsites 85 and 86. It begins by following the river for 100 m before travelling an old skidder road until it heads up and over the little rise. From here a short drop leads to the lakeside trail where a left turn and few metres takes you to the swimming area. On a hot day you will welcome the chance to go for a swim in the relatively warm water.

The lakeshore trail makes a pleasant walk around One Mile Lake between dips and takes well under an hour.

Lillooet River Dikes

Flat walk ... Views ... Wild animals ... River ... Biking

A walk along the dike of the Lillooet River with incredible views of Mt. Currie. Signs of many animals found in the valley abound along the edge of the dike.

Trail length: 4 km to turnaround spot
Walking time: 3 hours return

Location: Between Pemberton and Mount Currie village
45 minute drive from Whistler

Driving distance from Whistler Village: 34.0 km

Driving instructions: From Whistler Village, drive 31.9 km north on Highway 99 to a T-junction. Turn right on the D'Arcy road and drive 2.1 km to the bridge over the Lillooet. Park off the road. The route starts on the Mount Currie (east) side of the bridge.

 Hiking: A flat walk on a well defined route.

 Wheelchairs: An ideal grade although not paved.

 Mountain biking: Good ride for kids. The dike continues on to give a route to a bridge on the upper Lillooet road, creating a circle route of 50 flat km.

 Cross-country skiing: Perfect ski trip for young children, but the season is short.

 Fishing: Fishing for rainbow trout off the dike.

Picnicking: No picnic tables but lots of big boulders.

 **Natural history:** Game sign, especially deer and beaver, everywhere.

"Oh, the boredom of walking a river dike." Well, it doesn't apply in this case. The Lillooet River dikes present ever-changing views of scenery and rural life with the possibility of seeing some of the many forms of wildlife found in the area.

Starting on the Mount Currie village (east) side of the Lillooet River bridge, walk upriver along the dike to the B.C. Rail tracks. If you look back you can see spectacular Mt. Currie towering above you with the river flowing in the foreground. Mt. Everest is 8848 m high and rises 3500 m above its base; Mt. Currie is 2596 m high but rises 2300 m above its base, over two-thirds that of Everest. One of the interesting aspects of the Coast Mountains is that although the mountains are not particularly high, the relief (elevation differential between the base and the top) is among the greatest in the world.

Lillooet River dikes

59

As you walk up the dike keep an eye on the ground for deer and bear sign and on the trees for evidence of beaver. Deer and bear leave footprints to mark their passing, but beavers leave gnawed trees and pointed stumps to mark their work.

Across the river you will see signs of logging and farming, the major economic activities in the valley. The rumble of logging trucks on the nearby road, the cutblocks on the mountain sides, and the expanse of massive trees are obvious indicators of the economic importance of logging. The Pemberton Valley is a important source of seed potatoes, because the surrounding mountains and unseen Lillooet Lake create a naturally isolated agricultural area that acts to quarantine plants when strict importation rules are followed.

Cross the tracks into the woods and follow an old road. Soon you reach a large swamp, a perfect habitat for moose and duck. Take time to look for them before continuing. From here the route continues upriver along the edge of the valley. With the woodlands on your right, now is a good opportunity to see the life under the trees. In a few hundred metres you pass an old cabin, and as you come into view of a house, a faint road leads out to the river. This is a good place to enjoy a sandwich and the view. After lunch turn around and retrace your route.

Murphy in the Outdoors

No matter how carefully and how many times you check your list you will forget something. And it will be the thing you need the most.

The phrase "You can't miss it" guarantees that you will.

Good weather doesn't last, bad weather does.

"Waterproof clothing" is a contradiction in terms.

Lillooet Lake Walks

Short lakeshore walks... Camping... Picnicking...
Canoeing... Fishing... Ice-cold swimming... Views

A series of B.C. Forest Service campsites on the edge of Lillooet Lake, each with a walk along the lakeshore and with great views of the surrounding mountains.

Trail length: 2.5 km or less
Hiking time: 1 hour

Location: On the east side of Lillooet Lake
75 minutes from Whistler Village

Driving distance from Whistler Village: 55.0–65.1 km
39.5 km highway
15.5–25.6 km gravel road

Driving instructions: From Whistler Village, drive 31.9 km north to T-junction. Turn right and go along the D'Arcy road for 6.6 km. Turn right at the church in Mount Currie onto the Duffey Lake road. At 10.0 km take the right fork down Lillooet Lake east road. The B.C. Forest Service campsites are:
Strawberry Point: 6.5 km
Twin One: 9.7 km
Lizzie Bay: 14.8 km
Driftwood Bay: 16.6 km

 Hiking: Short, easy walks along the edge of the lake.

 Swimming: Extremely cold water, but good safe beaches for children.

 Canoeing: Good, but be wary of winds that pick up quickly and make the lake very dangerous.

Picnicking: Four great areas with a limited number of tables.

Camping: Four B.C. Forest Service areas. User-maintained, limited room.

Hiking the shoreline at Lizzie Bay

On a sunny summer's day, the four B.C. Forest Service campsites on the eastern edge of Lillooet Lake offer pleasant family outings with a wide variety of things to do. Access is straightforward: drive down the good gravel road on the east side of Lillooet Lake until you reach the campsite of your choice. Turn off at the posted sign and a very short drive will have you parked beside a picnic table.

The walks follow the shoreline and are marked if they wander off it into the woods. The beaches are sandy for the most part with the occasional rocky section. The walks go to the farthest part of the point they are located on, usually where a stream prevents further progress. Avoid the temptation to jump from rock to rock over to the other side as it is very easy to slip and take a bad spill. Just content yourself with admiring the views and studying the woodland life along the edge of shore.

Leave your swimming to a warmer lake, because Lillooet Lake is very cold. The lake is fed almost entirely by rivers that consist of freshly melted snow and ice.

The lake is a good place for canoeing, but stay close to shore. The wind gets up very quickly, and the water becomes extremely choppy and dangerous as the valley funnels the wind down the lake.

So pick a campsite and enjoy a picnic, or camp and enjoy the sunset.

On the final approach to the Black Tusk

Hikes

The Whistler region offers such a large number of excellent hikes that selecting only a few of the best is a highly personal and difficult task. I've chosen hikes that head for the prettiest and most interesting scenery in the area. These trips range from those that the whole family will enjoy to stiff hikes for experienced hikers. At least half the hikes are day trips for most people while the other half are nicer and more realistically done as overnight trips. You don't need much in the way of skills and equipment for most of these trips. For the day trips carry a pack with some lunch, a waterbottle, and a sweater and rain jacket. A pair of light hiking boots is adequate for all these trips, but the shorter ones only require walking shoes. It's always a good idea to take a map and compass.

Although these trails are basically straightforward and there is little in the way of obvious danger, they are wilderness trails in a wilderness environment and as such can be extremely dangerous if not treated with respect.

Now take a hike.

Squamish Chief

Viewpoint extraordinaire ... Seascapes ... Mountain vista ...
Fjords ...

A steep trail to a viewpoint 640 m above Howe Sound that looks into the mountains. The hiker can ascend the south peak or do a loop that crosses over the central and north peaks.

Trail length: 8 km return
Hiking time: 3 hour return if only doing one peak
Elevation gain: 600 m

Location: Squamish
  60 minute drive from Whistler Village
  60 minutes from Vancouver

Driving distance from Whistler Village: 59.6 km

Driving instructions: From Whistler Village, drive 59.6 km south on Highway 99 to a viewpoint on the left (east) side. Drive through gap at the back and turn right on an old road; follow it 1.0 km to parking area.

 Hiking: Easy but steep hikes to the summits.

 Rock climbing: Canada's rock climbing centre.

 Natural wonders: Coastal mountain and fjord scenery.

The Stawamus Chief, more commonly known as the Squamish Chief or simply the Chief, is the great monolith of granite that looms above the Highway 99 just south of Squamish. Its fame as Canada's premier rock climbing centre gives it world-wide acclaim, but its local popularity is equally due to the backside trail that leads hikers to the top and magnificent views of Howe Sound and the Squamish valley.

Before you leave the viewpoint beside Highway 99, there are a few features you should notice on the front side of the Chief. Off to the left is a large area of 45° rock that descends almost to the highway. These slabs are called the Apron and, with the Little Smoke Bluffs (page 51) that appear in the distance just behind them, represent the most popular rock climbing areas on the Chief (page 170).

A second feature is the black line running up the face directly in front of you. This feature, called a dike, was formed by molten rock filling a crack in the pre-existing granite. The dike sports an extremely difficult route called, appropriately, the Black Dyke.

If you look along the base of the face to the left of the Black Dyke you will see a triangular flake of rock, called the Flake, leaning against the main face. The Grand Wall route, the original line up the face, begins here. It was climbed in 1961 by Jim Baldwin and Ed Cooper and signalled the beginning of the Chief's fame as a rock climbing centre. If you look above the Flake on a summer's day you will probably see climbers, as the Grand Wall is the most popular route on the big walls of the Chief.

Smooth slabs and great views from the top of the Chief   Photo by John Clarke

The hiking trail gives an easier and safe way to the top of the Chief. The trail starts up wooden stairs at the end of the old road. About ten minutes up the stairs, a spur leads out over the creek to a trail leading to Shannon Falls. The Chief trail itself climbs steeply from the bridge to a fork. The right branch goes to the central and north peaks and the left fork goes to the south peak.

Most people take the left fork to the south peak, because it is the shortest route and has the most spectacular views. This trail switchbacks steeply before easing off near the summit. Although the angle lessens, the amount of care needed increases because you are walking across smooth slabs and it is a long way down.

The right branch of the trail continues to a second fork. It's best to go left at this second fork to the gap between the south and central peaks, because it is easier to scramble up the rock to the central peak than it is to descend it. Once on the central peak it is easiest to continue over the summit to the gap between it and the north peak. From this gap you can either traverse the north peak (the highest of the three summits) or descend directly to rejoin the main trail. Regardless of which route you take, you will have an invigorating hike with splendid views.

Once on the top take a look around at the views, then look down at Squamish and Highway 99. If you are on the south peak, you are standing at the top of the Grand Wall route, which you saw from below. From any of the peaks, resist the temptation to go near the edge and roll rocks down. It drops very(!) suddenly for a very long distance, and there are climbers below.

Retrace your steps carefully to the fork, where you can head up to the other summits or return to your car.

Diamond Head

Popular alpine area . . . Alpine flowers, meadows and lakes . . .
Easy overnight trip . . . Cross-country skiing . . . Wilderness
camping . . . Spectacular close-up views of Mt. Garibaldi

A gentle hike up an old gravel road gives easy, straightforward access to a beautiful alpine region. The naturalist's cabin at Elfin Lakes provides a centre from which to explore the meadows and volcanic features, and to view the mountain scenery that surrounds the area.

Trail length: 11 km one way
Hiking time: 7 hours return
Elevation gain: 880 m

Location: North of Squamish
   60 minute drive from Whistler
   90 minute drive from Vancouver

Driving distance from Whistler Village: 68.8 km
   54.8 km highway
   14 km narrow gravel road

Driving instructions: From Whistler Village, drive 52.8 km south on Highway 99 and turn left. Stay on the main road, which turns into a narrow gravel logging road in 2 km. Go left at the fork in the gravel road, and continue to the parking lot. It is 16 km from the turnoff to the parking lot. The road is steep and chains are required in winter.

Selected hikes: From Elfin Lakes:
   Gargoyle Col: scenery and volcanic features, 4 hours return
   Opal Cone: volcanic features close-up, 4 hours return

Accommodation: Red Heather (2 hours from parking lot): shelter with wilderness camping
   Elfin Lakes: public cabin, and restricted camping

Information: Park naturalist at Elfin Lakes in the summer. Brochures available at parking lot.

Hiking: The alpine area has many easy, well-marked trails.

 Climbing: Access to Garibaldi and Mamquam mountains.

 Cross-country skiing: Good intermediate skiing, especially in the area between Red Heather shelter and the Gargoyle Col. Avalanche danger in this area. The Elfin Lake cabin is the start of the Garibaldi Névé traverse (p. 175).

 Mountain biking: Only on the jeep track to Elfin Lakes cabin.

 Swimming: Bracing dips available in Elfin Lakes.

 Natural wonders: Spectacular volcanic features, glaciers, and magnificent mountain scenery are highly visible and easily reached.

Diamond Head is one of the most popular outdoor recreation areas in the Whistler region because of the many activities available to everyone, beginner and expert, summer and winter. For hikers, this trip is best in August and September, as snow often lingers in the alpine until late July.

From the parking lot hike along a jeep road to Elfin Lakes, which is both a destination in itself and a centre of operations. For the first thirty minutes the road climbs steeply before making a few gentle sweeping switchbacks to the Red Heather shelter at the edge of the alpine meadows. This point, near the halfway mark and about two hours from the parking lot, makes a pleasant lunch stop because you have just left the trees and the views are magnificent. If you've had a late start (like after dinner in Whistler) this is a good place to stop and camp.

Above the shelter the road switchbacks a few more times to the top of Paul Ridge. Here Mt. Garibaldi dominates the skyline. This massive peak with three summits is named for the Italian patriot, Giuseppe Garibaldi. It was this landmark, so conspicuous from Howe Sound, that attracted mountaineers near the turn of the century and ultimately led to the creation of Garibaldi Provincial Park in 1920. The park currently covers 195 000 hectares between Squamish and Pemberton. The Diamond Head of Garibaldi Park is the southern summit of the mountain, which has a

First view of Elfin Lakes

pyramidal shape and hides the higher northern summits when seen from Squamish.

Once on Paul Ridge, follow the road in its winding descent to the cabin at Elfin Lakes. In the winter the trail, marked by poles, goes behind the ridge to avoid the avalanche areas on the west side.

At Elfin Lakes there is a large open-area cabin available for public use, and 300 m away is a wilderness campground. The hike from parking lot to cabin takes about four hours, depending on your pace and the number of stops.

Many hikes can be done from here. One of the best is up to Gargoyle Col, the prominent notch in the ridge between Columnar Peak and the Gargoyles. This pass gives impressive views of Diamond Head and the Squamish valley. Pick up the trail by continuing along the jeep road past the campsite to where a marked trail branches left and heads up the hillside. This col is a marvellous place to gain an insight into the volcanic activity that shaped this corner of Garibaldi Park. Mt. Garibaldi is a volcanic peak that last erupted about 12 000 years ago (yesterday in geological time). This eruption occurred near the end of the last ice age when there was still kilometre-deep ice in the Squamish valley. The lava (molten rock) was dammed up by the ice that then filled the Squamish valley. When the ice melted, the entire western side of the mountain collapsed into the valley a thousand metres below. It is estimated that about 3 cubic kilometres of rock went down into the Squamish valley. Even today the rock on the face of Diamond Head continues slowly but steadily to disintegrate. This constant fall of rock ensures that the only time that climbers venture onto this spectacular mountain face is in the winter when snow and ice holds the rocks together.

Another popular trip from the cabin follows the jeep track as it continues up toward the Garibaldi Névé. The névé is the large area of ice that you see at the head of Ring Creek. This is the start of the Garibaldi Névé traverse. Here you can get a close look at a very recent volcano, Opal Cone. If you scramble up the lava ridge north of the Ring Creek bridge and walk up it to the meadows you can make your way to the rim of the crater. The crater itself is about 300 m across and 10 m deep. It is hard to imagine that this small thing sent a flow of lava 17 km long down Ring Creek to within a few kilometres of where Highway 99 is now. The total amount of lava that came out of the crater was over 6 cubic kilometres, or about twice that of the 1980 Mt. St. Helens eruption, and equivalent to a cube 2 km by 3 km standing a kilometre high. That would be a 10 km run around a very tall rock.

In the winter, the relatively gentle terrain makes the area ideal for the beginning back-country skier. The cabin at Elfin Lakes makes a good destination for your first trip with a pack.

It very important to remember that the descent on skis from the high point on Paul Ridge to the cars is long and steep and potentially dangerous. Tired skiers, especially beginners, should go slowly and be able to turn and stop properly. If you doubt your abilities, walk down but stay on the edge of the trail out of respect for others.

Black Tusk

Alpine meadows... Scenery... Lakes... Flowers... Vistas...
Wilderness camping... Cross-country skiing

A well graded trail leads to a splendid alpine playground that has unlimited opportunities for enjoyment. Although a great day trip, this area is better enjoyed by staying overnight.

The Tusk is a stiff scramble with marvellous views. The many trails in the meadows provide the chance to explore the entire area.

Trail length: 21 km return
Hiking time: 8 hours required for loop
Elevation gain: 1050 m

Location: South of Whistler
30 minutes drive from Whistler Village
2 hours from Vancouver

Driving distance from Whistler Village: 27.0 km

Driving instructions: From Whistler Village, drive south 24.6 km on Highway 99. Take the Black Tusk turnoff on the left and drive 2.4 km to the parking lot.

 Hiking: Excellent trail to the alpine, and kilometres of trails in the alpine meadows.

 Swimming: The smaller lakes provide good swimming.

 Camping: Good campsites in the summer. The shelters at Battleship Islands are open for winter use.

 Fishing: Rainbow trout are found in Garibaldi Lake.

Climbing: Black Tusk is a stiff scramble. Serious alpine climbing is available on the far side of Garibaldi Lake.

 Cross-country skiing: Excellent intermediate skiing, but climbing and descending the Barrier requires skins and care.

 Mountain biking: Not permitted.

 Natural wonders: Alpine meadows and flowers, volcanic rocks, and mountains vistas above a huge alpine lake.

Visitors to the Black Tusk area have almost too many things to do during a short stay. You can spend days and days based out of the campsites by Battleship Islands and Taylor Meadows, yet leave still not having seen or done everything there is to do in this wonderful area.

Regardless of how long you spend here you must start by hiking up the Barrier. The trail, probably the best in southwestern B.C., starts with a steady ascent as it follows Rubble Creek back towards the Barrier. At the 2 km mark the trail starts to switchback up the Barrier. Although the grade is very gentle, sometimes too gentle, avoid taking short cuts as they cause erosion.

About halfway up, there is a good view of the Barrier at close range. This impressive cliff formed when the hot lava from an eruption of Mt. Price was dammed up by ice of the last ice age, about 12 000 years ago. The rock slope that you look across resulted from a landslide in 1856. The slide carried debris all the way down to the Cheakamus River nearly 5 km distant.

It takes the trail 6 km to reach the top the Barrier. The terrain begins to level out and the trail splits. You can go left to Taylor campsite and the Black Tusk Meadows, or right to Battleship Islands campsite and Garibaldi Lake. It is a toss-up. If you are out on a day trip you are best off going left and looping around Taylor and down Parnassus Creek, just beyond it, to Garibaldi Lake and back to the junction.

If you are staying any length of time, Taylor is the best centre for a variety of excursions. However, the Battleship Islands are so scenic that you should spend a night there. From Taylor campsite you can see the extinct volcano of Black Tusk to the north. You might consider scrambling up to the base of it for the views alone. If you have some athletic ability and don't mind heights, the climb to the summit is a worthwhile

Evening light on Garibaldi Lake from Battleship Islands

and unforgettable experience. If you do decide to climb the Tusk, take great care. The first 50 m involve some easy climbing up a gully. The rock in the gully and on the Tusk tends to be loose, so be careful. Above the chimney the terrain becomes easier as you approach the summit. Actually the highest summit is across a gap and only a metre higher. But the ascent requires proper climbing gear and so is only done by experienced climbers. On the descent it is even easier to knock rocks down and the last chimney is difficult to find, so be extra careful.

Another popular trip from Taylor is the walk up to Black Tusk and Mimulus lakes. This is a pleasant romp in the meadows with the added possibility of a swim in warm water. Trails radiate out from these lakes in many directions. It is worth taking the time to investigate some of them. The park naturalist based in Taylor in the summer will be glad to recommend hikes and to answer questions you might have about the area.

A visit to Battleship Islands is mandatory for the views across Garibaldi Lake. The lake is over 200 m deep. This depth is the result of the wall that formed when the molten lava of the Barrier hit the ice and cooled. As this wall blocked the only outlet for the water, the valley behind it filled to create Garibaldi Lake.

The trail from Garibaldi Lake to the top of the Barrier passes several lakes. There is no surface outlet for these lakes; they drain underground through the porous rocks of the Barrier into Rubble Creek.

In the winter the Battleship Islands are a popular camping area. The shelters here provide access to the Sphinx cabin and an exit for those doing the Garibaldi Névé traverse (page 175). The ascent, because of the steady steep climb, and the descent, because of the sharp turns, are best done wearing skins on your skis. If you decide to visit the area in the winter, please don't walk up the trail as your footprints ruin the path for skiing.

But here we were completely alone, the silence ringing in our ears like church bells. Here we were free from the artifice of society and the land was free from the ravages of industry. Here we could experience wildlands whole and complete, and claim their wholeness as part of our own. Here we could commune with the wilderness, silent and peaceful, yet powerful and unyielding, and draw strength from it as if drinking from the spring of eternal life. Here we could feel the rhythm and spirit of Nature unblemished by the invasions of man, feel that cleansing and renewal of the soul that comes with being in these uplifted places still whole and complete as the creator first made them.

That feeling doesn't come instantly. You can't step out of a helicopter in the middle of nowhere and immediately be fully involved in a wilderness experience. The feeling grows slowly, gathering the body with the passage of time like fine wine coming of age. You need to be out there in the wilderness for a while, just being there, just listening, just staying still.

You also get that feeling by moving through wilderness, especially a big wilderness, travelling and taking in a great expanse of wild country where the forces of Nature go their way undisturbed. As you move through wilderness and walk its diversity, you begin to take in its pattern and flow. Time, as we measure the frenzied dash of our daily lives, slows, becomes almost suspended. You enter into the rapture of wilderness space-time, where one feels connected with something much greater than oneself, and in humbleness becomes that much more open to the joy and beauty of Creation.

Coast Range climbs especially hold this mystique because Coast country is still so wild, remote, and pristine. This is the enchantment that draws me back time after time.

Michael Down
Canadian Alpine Journal, 1990

Singing Pass

Alpine meadows . . . Gentle hiking . . . Cascading glaciers . . .
Rugged mountain peaks . . . Whistler Village's back yard

Ascends the side of Whistler Mountain to Singing Pass between and behind Whistler and Blackcomb mountains. The pass provides spectacular views of Garibaldi Park, particularly the Black Tusk area. The alpine area offers a variety of biotic sub-zones and a mix of flowers to match.

Trail length: 18 km return
Hiking time: 7 hours return to Russet Lake cabin
Elevation gain: 800 m

Location: Between Whistler and Blackcomb mountains
15 minute drive from Whistler Village

Driving distance from Whistler Village: 5 km gravel

Driving instructions: From Whistler Village, drive toward the Blackcomb ski lifts. Just before crossing Fitzsimmons Creek turn right up a narrow gravel road. Follow this 4.8 km to the end and limited parking.

Accommodation: Small public shelter with limited room.

 Hiking: Excellent trail at a reasonable grade. Experts can combine this hike with a journey over the Musical Bumps from Whistler Mountain ski area for a loop trip.

 Climbing: Easy glacier and alpine climbs available behind the cabin.

 Cross-country skiing: Often used by expert backcountry skiers to descend from the Spearhead traverse.

Swimming: Only for the brave.

 Mountain biking: Not permitted.

 Natural wonders: Alpine meadows, vistas of cascading glaciers, and glacier-hung peaks at close range.

The trail starts from the parking lot by climbing an old mining road for a kilometre to an old abandoned mine. Here old train tracks hang over the edge and it is possible to walk a few metres into the mine entrance to the barricade that is there for safety reasons.

Shortly past the mine the road degenerates into an excellent trail. The gentle grade ascends the hillside above Fitzsimmons Creek past Harmony, Flute, and Oboe creeks through a noble forest of mature timber that is humdrum as far as scenic views are concerned but undeniably alluring.

As the trail swings up into Melody Creek it leaves the forest and enters first the subalpine zone then the alpine meadows. These are a myriad of colours in the latter part of August. On the surface this looks like a single area with flowers growing anywhere and everywhere. Of course, Mother Nature never allows such randomness and with some looking (and Singing Pass is a great place to do it) you will see an orderly series of sub-zones. Please keep on the trails in the meadow areas, as these meadows are fragile. Oh, yeah – bring a flower book.

Like the Black Tusk meadows, the leas (this word for meadows is a crossword favourite) in the pass itself are moist or seep meadows. These fields occur at the base of high uplands, from which they get a renewal of nutrients from the water that drains the ground above. Here you will find mimulus, lupines, hellebores, orchids, and numerous other flowers. You'll be glad you brought that flower book!

Open, flatter meadows do not exist here but are found at Rainbow Lake (page 83) and Warner Pass (page 189). These meadows are dry and not as nutrient-rich and are dominated by Indian paintbrush and arnicas, with lupines and valerian being found in the slightly moister areas. Don't forget a flower book or you'll be mad at yourself.

As you hike up the slope to the Russet Lake you pass through sedge meadows, which are not surprisingly dominated by sedge. Because the soils here are more porous and stonier than those below, the only plants that can survive are those that can withstand drier conditions. Paintbrush, mountain daisies, and fleabane are the common flowering plants in this area. Are you mad or happy at yourself? Think flower book.

The ridge crest above Russet Lake is a sub-glacial fell-field, a fancy term for a stony area. Here the soil is scarce and thin and the weather harsh, so cushion plants dominate. These are characterized by round streamlined shapes that help them survive the constant winds. The bun-like shape allows the plant to absorb and retain more heat, which keeps the roots warmer. Plants here are few and far between, because the area needed by each plant to absorb the water required for growth is large. The showy flowers attract the few insects that live here.

Continue down the path to the Russet Lake cabin, which is further away than it looks but not all that far in reality. The extra walk is worthwhile as the cabin sits on the edge of a hanging valley looking down into the Municipality of Whistler.

First class accommodations at the hotel at Russet Lake

Wedgemount Lake

Glacier descending to the lakeshore . . . Mountain panorama

An exceedingly steep trail leads to a large lake above timberline with a glacier descending to its shore. A short walk over rocky terrain leads to the side of the glacier.

Trail length: 6 km one way
Hiking time: 8 hours return to Wedgemount cabin
Elevation gain: 1280 m

Location: Whistler Municipality
15 minutes from Whistler Village

Driving distance from Whistler Village: 13.8 km
12.1 km highway
1.7 km narrow gravel road

Driving instructions: From Whistler Village, drive 12.1 km north on Highway 99. Turn right, cross the railroad tracks and a bridge, then turn left. Go right, left, and continue another 1.7 km to the parking lot.

 Hiking: An extremely steep trail from bottom to top.

 Climbing: A favourite local haunt.

 Natural wonders: A glacier descending to the lakeshore.

There is nothing in the mountain world that quite matches the splendour of a glacier entering a lake, and that was the glory of Wedgemount Lake until the end of the 1980s. If you don't mind an extremely, almost obscenely, steep hike then this the opportunity of a lifetime.

The trail starts behind the sign in the parking lot and gradually ascends through the logging slash to meet Wedgemount Creek and the old-growth timber at the same time. Here, twenty minutes from the car, the trail crosses Wedgemount Creek. Fill your waterbottle here, as it is a long, steep haul to the next water. On the other side of the creek, the path switchbacks up the embankment and then follows Wedgemount Creek. The trail heads for a climber's hut, and the steepness of the trail suggests its original purpose. The trail crosses one rockslide early on and a second one about half way up. Although water is available at the start of the second slide, it is somewhat stagnant. Better water is found in the babbling rills that are a few minutes beyond the far side of the slide. The trail flattens as it passes the rills until it almost goes into a small brook. Here it makes a sharp left turn and starts to climb steeply again.

Somewhere along this stretch stop and fill your waterbottle again, as this is the last water before treeline. And you might do well to have a bite to eat, as the trail from here on makes what you have already done seem flat. Not only does it steepen but it steepens even more as it gets higher.

About a quarter hour after restarting, you will see a substantial waterfall on your right. The top of the waterfall is level with Wedgemount Lake and your goal, the cabin, is 50 m above that. Unfortunately the horizontal distance is not much more than what you can see. As you enter the subalpine the trail traverses scree slopes before starting its final climb. A short stop is probably a good idea before starting this final 30-minute section. The angle gets progressively steeper until it seems nearly vertical, but once at the top it is a 5-minute, slightly downhill walk to the cabin. As the cabin is small, bring a tent if you are staying overnight.

After a good rest and feed and a look at the utterly magnificent views, a walk along the lakeshore to the snout of the Wedgemount Glacier is more than worthwhile. Because of the interesting sights and the deceiving length of the walk, allow two hours for the round trip.

A century and a half ago the glacier reached a point directly below the cabin. However, the warming trend that began in the 1850s has caused the glacier to retreat nearly 1.5 km. The rocks you cross to reach the lakeshore were left by the glacier as it retreated. The ground along the lakeshore is glacial silt, formed by the grinding of rock on rock under the glacier to create a fine sand. If you fill a waterbottle up here you will notice the water is cloudy because of the silt in the water. Leave it to sit while you wander up to the glacier's snout, and by your return the silt will have settled to the bottom and the water will be clear.

The path to the snout of the glacier is flanked by the lakeshore on one side and a lateral moraine on the other. The unvegetated part of this moraine was covered by ice until relatively recently and shows how thick the glacier was. At the snout of the glacier you can see into some of the crevasses. *Do not* wander onto the glacier unless you are properly equipped, as glaciers and crevasses are potentially hazardous.

Until the very late 1980s the glacier actually entered the lake. In recent decades, hot summers and the lack of heavy snowfall have caused the glacier to melt faster than it is advancing. The result is that the glacier no longer reaches the lake. If you take the number of years since 1987 and divide that into the distance the snout is from the lake you will know how many metres per year on average the glacier is retreating.

The descent to your car follows the ascent route. In many ways the trip out is harder on the body than the ascent because of its steepness. Take special care descending the top steep section as the gravel and dirt on the trail cover smooth rock, making it easy to slip. Once in the woods be careful not to get up too much speed. The many roots and rocks that stick out make it easy to trip and do substantial harm to yourself.

Air photos looking straight down on Wedgemount Lake. Note how the glacier has retreated between 1951 (left) and 1987 (right). Photos courtesy of B.C. Institute of Technology

Rainbow Lake

Meadows . . . Lakes . . . Fishing . . . Swimming

A trail on the western side of the Whistler valley that ascends through the woods to a large lake in rolling alpine country with views back into the Whistler ski areas.

Trail length: 16 km return
Hiking time: 6 hours return to Rainbow Lake
Elevation gain: 850 m

Location: Whistler Municipality
  15 minutes from Whistler Village

Driving distance from Whistler Village: 7.1 km

Driving instructions: From Whistler Village, drive north 3.9 km on Highway 99 to the Alpine Meadows turnoff. Turn left onto Rainbow Drive then take first left onto Alta Lake Road. After 3.2 km, a sign on the right (west side) marks the start of the trail.

 Hiking: Moderate hike to the lake, with strolling possible in the alpine meadows.

 Swimming: Good swimming, especially in the smaller tarns.

 Fishing: The lake is stocked with rainbow trout.

 Camping: Wilderness camping.

If you want views back across the Whistler valley to the ski slopes on Whistler and Blackcomb, then the hike to Rainbow Lake will give you what you are looking for, plus the chance to wander in alpine meadows. In a way, this hike is a strange one in that there is nothing special, spectacular or particularly memorable about it, yet it draws people back again and again, as it will you.

The trail starts by ascending the side of Twentyone Mile Creek. Part way up this trail it's worthwhile to make a short side trip to view Rainbow Falls. After about ten minutes the trail comes out onto a road that it follows uphill for about twenty minutes until the road peters out into a trail. The road is washed out in places, making it difficult to get by.

As the trail restarts, it ascends steeply through the old logging slash and into the timber where its angle eases. The trail ascends gently through the timber up into the subalpine on a series of boardwalks. This trail probably has more boardwalks than the rest of the Coast Mountains combined. Upon leaving the forest, boardwalks lead across the extensive marshy areas. Finally you cross Twentyone Mile Creek, which in days past was the scene of many a misadventure on the boulder-hopping crossing of the creek. Now a bridge avoids this fun exercise.

On the other side of the creek, a short steep ascent leads to Rainbow Lake. Here you can swim and relax before taking a stroll around the lake or into the surrounding meadows.

If you continue beyond the lake (the north side is the best) to the low pass at the opposite end, you can look down on other small tarns that, like Rainbow, were formed in the last ice age by glaciers gouging out the rocks. During the last century Rainbow has shrunk in size and depth because the glacier and snowfall on which it relies for its water have shrunk in size and amount.

As you re-enter the logging slash on your descent, Wedge Mountain on the far side of the Whistler valley dominates the view. Without looking at a map, try to guess which mountain is Wedge – it's not hard.

Joffre Lakes

Three azure lakes ... Icefall ... Mountain peaks

A moderate hike that features three cobalt-blue lakes backed by a spectacular icefall. The first lake is five easy minutes from the car. The middle and upper lakes require more effort but are well worth it.

Trail length: 12 km return
Hiking time: 5 hours return to Upper Joffre Lake
Elevation gain: 400 m

Location: Duffey Lake road
   60 minute drive from Whistler Village

Driving distance from Whistler Village: 61.1 km
   52.0 km highway
   9.1 km gravel

Driving instructions: From Whistler Village, drive 31.9 km north on Highway 99. Take a right at T-junction and drive 6.6 km to Duffey Lake road turnoff. Drive 22.6 km along Duffey Lake road to Joffre Lakes Alpine Recreational Area. Turn right into the parking lot where the trail starts.

 Hiking: A moderate hike of medium length.

 Climbing: A major alpine mountaineering centre.

 Fishing: The lakes are stocked with rainbow trout.

 Swimming: Icy, only for those with no nerves in their skin.

 Natural wonders: Glaciers and glacier-created features.

As you approach the high point on the Duffey Lake road, 22.6 km from Mount Currie village, a sign on the right marks the parking lot for the Joffre Lakes Recreational Area. The start of the trail is signposted. When the trail forks after a hundred metres, going straight ahead for a short distance will put you on the shore of Lower Joffre Lake. Here a stupendous view of a turquoise lake surrounded by an evergreen muff topped by glacial white will greet you.

Return to the fork and head up the trail to the other lakes. After crossing Joffre Creek where it exits Lower Joffre Lake, the trail climbs slowly and steadily before dropping to the edge of the incoming creek. The trail picks its way up through rock slide, and gradually steepens until

This view of Slalok Peak from Lower Joffre Lake is only five minutes from your car.

just before Middle Joffre Lake. The trail now levels off and follows the creek to the lake where it crosses the creek on a couple of logs. Here again the view is breathtaking.

The trail hugs the shore until it reaches the creek flowing into the far end of the middle lake. The trail now climbs very steeply but it quickly levels out and continues to Upper Joffre Lake. This is the most magnificent of the three lakes, with the glacier suspended right above it. The trail continues along the right (south) shore to the picnic sites at Tszil Creek. The nicest picnic spots are on sandy beaches along the lake shore. Although there are short walks available in the area, the region beyond the lake is best left to mountaineers.

The blue colour of the lake is caused by fine rock particles that are brought down from the glacier by the water as the ice melts. The glacial silt, as it is called, causes the water to reflect different wavelengths of light than water normally does, giving a glacial lake its unusual blue colour.

From your picnic spot, the Matier Glacier will pull your eyes away from the glorious blue of the lake. The Matier Glacier is a hanging glacier, so named because it hangs on the cliffs above the lake. It presents a great danger to mountaineers because chunks of ice may break off without warning as they cross beneath the cliffs. Stay well away from the cliffs if you decide to wander around the lake.

If you are lucky you will see a chunk of ice come hurtling down. The large pinnacles you see in the glacier as it approaches the cliffs are called seracs. These pillars of ice form as the glacier is pulled apart and broken up. As you sit at the lake you will probably hear seracs falling, but it's unlikely that you will be able to see them.

Lizzie Meadows

Alpine meadows . . . Mountain tarns . . . More alpine meadows . . .
More mountain tarns . . . Mountain strolls

If you like tarns and meadows this area has an unlimited supply of both.
The trail to the alpine meadows and the trails in the meadows have short,
steep, rugged sections. The meadows and tarns beyond the camping area
are easily reached and very inviting.

Trail length: 5 km one way
Hiking time: 6 hours return from the road
Elevation gain: 260 m

Location: East side of Lillooet Lake
75 minutes from Whistler Village

Driving distance from Whistler Village: 77.1 km
39.4 km highway
37.7 km gravel

Driving instructions: From Whistler Village, drive 31.9 km north on
Highway 99. Go right at the T-junction and drive 6.6 km to the
Duffey Lake road turnoff. Drive 10.0 km to the Lillooet Lake
road turnoff. Follow this gravel road for 17.7 km and turn left up
a logging road immediately before a bridge. Stay on the main
branch for 7.9 km, then take the next two left forks and climb a
steep hill before parallelling Lizzie Creek. You might want to park
here as the hill is steep and rough; if you do, park well off the
road. This will add about an hour to your hiking time. The main
parking area is at 10.9 km.

 Hiking: Numerous hikes and scrambles of varying length and
difficulty range through the bevy of meadows and tarns. This
hike is the start of the Stein-Lizzie crossover.

 Swimming: An endless supply of tarns that are ideal for late
summer swimming.

Fishing: Rainbow in Long and Tundra lakes.

 Camping: Wilderness camping near the cabin.

 Cross-country skiing: Great skiing for experts but high avalanche hazard.

 Natural wonders: Alpine meadows and flowers in abundance, particularly in August.

Lizzie Meadows are known for easily accessible, wonderful alpine meadows and tarns. For lovers of alpine flowers and meadows, this is possibly the nicest hike in the region. Although you can do this trip as a pleasant day trip, you'll enjoy it even more if you can spend a couple of days here doing some of the many short hikes available and swimming in the many tarns.

From the parking area the trail heads into the woods for 100 m to a fork. The right fork takes you 100 m further to the shore of Lizzie Lake, and the left one leads to the meadows. The trail parallels the lake shore for a bit before starting to rise like a staircase, alternating steep and flat sections, then crosses a small scree slope as it passes through a narrow gorge into the subalpine zone. After wandering over a short section of flat terrain you reach a small log cabin on the upper edge of the subal pine zone.

A word of warning: the trail has many muddy sections, making good footwear essential. Please stay on the trail and go through the mud rather than around it in order to minimize the environmental damage. This is extra-important in the alpine meadows because they are super-sensitive to the passage of large organisms, and you are a large organism, and by going around the mud puddle you just increase its size and add to the erosion problem.

The cabin is open to the public but is very small. It's best to continue to the camping area about 50 m beyond. This serves as a nice base for the many short trips that are available.

The trail crosses the stream beside the camping area and ascends through the meadows. The main trail follows the creek in steep stretches up to Arrowhead Lake. The first step takes you up into the alpine zone. After a flat stretch, it ascends abruptly up a rockfield to Arrowhead Lake, where a bit of rock hopping takes you across the outlet creek to the other side of the lake.

Here you are in an expanse of alpine meadows that in August is abloom with many species of flowers. The brilliance of the meadows results from the short growing season, which begins when the snow melts and ends when the snow falls. In Lizzie Meadows that means from roughly the beginning of July to the end of September. The growing cycle of the plant has to be completed within at most three months, and most plants bank on a two month period, giving a bit of a safety margin. The result is that anything that is going to bloom has to do so by the end of August. Thus in the middle of August every plant is in full bloom and the slopes are a rainbow of colour.

Because of the short growing season, any damage to the meadows takes longer to repair than in areas with a longer growing seasons. Such destruction is not limited to the direct damage to the plants. The plant roots anchor the limited amount of soil; thus harming the plants results in greater soil erosion, which results in fewer plants growing, which in turn means less food for the animals, which means fewer animals, and so the trickle-down effect continues. In addition, because soil forms from organic matter, which is extremely slow to decay in this climate, the fewer the plants the less organic matter there is to decay and the slower the soil is replaced, beginning another vicious and related cycle. *Please remember that if the alpine meadows are to remain, you must help by minimizing damage to them and walk only on the established trails.*

The trail continues beyond Arrowhead Lake to the pass that looks down into the head of Rogers Creek. From the pass, you can scramble up to the summit of Tabletop Mountain to revel in the views, or you can continue around the headwaters of Rogers Creek to Caltha Lake, visible from the pass below Tabletop Mountain. From Caltha Lake you would do well to continue a little further to Tundra Lake and the headwaters of the Stein River. This point is the start of the Stein-Lizzie crossover (page 179).

If you are lazy or short on time, start up the trail to Arrowhead Lake. When you reach the first flat section walk a short distance and turn right up the slope. A path will take you up through a gully a short distance to a field of tarns above Long Lake. On a hot day in August these ponds are refreshingly cool. Because they are crystal clear you can safely dive into the deeper ones and avoid a slow painful descent into the cold water.

Mountain Biking

"Sea to Sky Country" need not be modest when it comes to describing its mountain biking terrain. Many think it is the best in the world, no ifs and buts about it. Nowhere else comes close. Can you name another area with this variety: pancake flat to super-steep, baby-bottom smooth to lunar rough, residential tour to wilderness expedition, from hour-long to never-ending, and from elementary schooler to daredevil terrain? All this is found in the spectacular mountain scenery right at your front door.

Because there are so many great trips in this area, it is hard to know where to start. Rather than describe all the possibilities – an impossible feat anyway – and take away the adventure that is the fun of mountain biking, I will describe only one road ride, one off-road ride, one mixed ride, and a short trip around Whistler. When you have done the trips recommended here and in Trip Ideas, make your own tour by choosing a starting point and then heading off along any road you fancy.

The Whistler-Pemberton area is a mountain biker's paradise, not only because it has mountains – many areas have those – but mountains with routes that give great riding. It is highly ironic that the logging roads, for all their ugliness, provide the finest mountain biking routes. These roads climb the steep mountain sides at angles that are rideable yet challenging. Unlike most hiking trails, which are rocky and crossed by logs, the roads are rough but bikeable. And above all there is an ever-changing number and variety of them to ride on, at skill levels from beginner to expert. So take your bike and explore.

Cycling in this region has all the usual dangers and problems of the sport anywhere and a few that are special to this area. Pack a proper repair kit, not only for the reasons you would elsewhere, but because when your bike breaks down, you are likely to find yourself up an un-travelled logging road. Wear a helmet. Also take a small repair kit for yourself containing band-aids, sunscreen, an antiseptic, and triangular bandage for larger wounds.

Cyclists should watch for hikers and yield the right of way to them. Respect for the environment and others using the trails will help you avoid angry shouting matches with irate hikers.

Some pointers on the terrain. The first and most important rule of the road (and the law in B.C.) is that cyclists must obey the same regula-tions as a motorist. The roads, even the paved ones, are nowhere near as smooth as they look. The curves tend to be sharper and longer than they look, so don't let yourself get up too much speed on the downhills regard-less of the temptation. Slow down even more on gravel roads. On gravel roads, water-filled potholes might be deeper than you think. The paved roads are greasy when wet, particularly after a dry spell. Because of the gravel shoulders and abrupt edges it is a good idea to cycle closer to the centre of the road than you might normally to avoid going off the pave-ment and having to make a sharp move back onto the road. This point is very important when a vehicle is passing you. Like a slow moving car, pull over and let traffic pass when it piles up behind you. Beware of back eddies when a vehicle passes you, particularly logging trucks or other large vehicles. Logging trucks are huge, hard to stop, and kick up amaz-ing clouds of dust on dry roads. When you are being passed by a logging truck on a gravel road it is best to get off your bike and wait a couple of minutes for following vehicles to get past you and the dust to settle. In general, take extra care and be extra courteous on logging roads.

Special mountain bike tours may be available on Whistler and Black-comb mountains using the ski lifts to get to the alpine areas. Ask at the base of the mountains for more information.

The safest approach to the routes beyond the boundaries of Whistler is the Valley Trail, which avoids having to cycle on Highway 99 while in Whistler. The winding nature of the roads makes them all dangerous to cycle on, but Highway 99 is by far the most dangerous because of the huge volume of traffic it carries.

Valley Trail (mostly paved)

This is part of the ever-expanding system of trails within the confines of the Municipality of Whistler. Starting at the underpass between the Village and the golf course, the trail winds south along the golf course to Alpha Lake, north to Alpine Meadows, and around Lost Lake with side routes around the golf course and to Rainbow Beach. This more-or-less flat trail is an ideal way to see Whistler and limits the amount of travel you have do on Highway 99 within Whistler. Families and those who just want an easy and relaxing ride should investigate this largely paved route. Pick up the latest map of this changing system at the visitor information centres and enjoy your tour of Whistler.

Cycling the Valley Trail

To reach the trail from Whistler Village, follow the road that takes the underpass beneath Highway 99 and goes to the golf course parking area. If you turn left in the parking lot, the trail takes you along the edge of the golf course, then through Alta Vista subdivision down to Lakeside Park on Alta Lake. From there the trail climbs and descends to Wayside Park at the southern end of Alta Lake before heading beside the train tracks to Nita Lake. The trail winds along the shore of Nita Lake, then past the train station to Alpha Lake Park, and out to the highway. Here you can retrace your route or cycle back on the highway. A compromise might be to do the half kilometre back to the gondola area on the highway, grab a drink at the store, then turn down Lake Placid Road and get back on the trail at Nita Lake.

If you make a right turn as you come out of the underpass, you can make a huge loop that takes you to Meadows Park on Green Lake, then to Lost Lake and finally back to the Village via the Blackcomb side. The route follows the edge of the golf course to the River of Golden Dreams. After crossing the river the route wanders through the woods beside the river towards Green Lake. There are two turnoffs to the left on this section. The first takes you around the Arnold Palmer Golf Course where you can join the south branch of the Valley Trail. The second turnoff takes you to Rainbow Beach, the best swimming spot on Alta Lake. Just before Meadows Park you can join the Alta Lake road, turn left and cycle along it to Highway 99 at the south end of Whistler, then go north to the south end of the Valley Trail. Continue north along the Valley Trail to where you cross the River of Golden Dreams on Highway 99. Here a gravel trail takes you down and along the edge of Green Lake, then around and through the new Green Lake Golf Course. After crossing the railway tracks, you go up Fitzsimmons Creek a short distance before crossing it and head up a hill to Lost Lake. The trail takes you around the northwestern side of Lost Lake to the parking lot, and from there you can return to Whistler Village by roads or the Lost Lake trails.

Lost Lake itself has over 25 km of connected trails. These undulating paths vary in relief between 50 and 100 m. With a good gravel surface they are ideal for the new trail rider and as a warmup for the expert. Cycle with great care, as walkers frequent the trails. Go through the parking lot and up the dirt road to the paved roads behind Blackcomb. Now just follow the road back to the Clock Tower.

Whichever way you go, this is a very relaxing and enjoyable cycle and method of seeing the Whistler valley.

Whistler-Pemberton Highway (paved)

Paved... Undulating downhill... Lakes... Rivers... Fishing...
Train ride

This lovely ride from Whistler to Pemberton has a net loss of elevation but is undulating enough to be interesting. You cycle past several lakes and rivers where you can stop and cool off or fish in. From Pemberton you can take the train back to Whistler to avoid having a steep ride back, or explore one of several alternative trips and routes.

Cycle length: 32.1 km one way
Elevation loss: 500 m
Cycling tIme: 3 hours

Route: Highway 99 between Whistler and Pemberton.

The directions for this road tour are simple: follow Highway 99 north from Whistler for 32.1 km to Pemberton. Although the route is obvious and has a net loss of elevation of 500 m, it is anything but a boring downhill run. The mountains prevent this straightforward route from being straight, and there is no such thing as a route that is all downhill regardless of the loss of elevation. Three hours is plenty of time to get yourself to Pemberton, but at least that much will be required again if you decide to cycle back.

Your journey starts by rolling through the northern half of Whistler, past the Wedgemount turnoff. This first section of the trip has the most traffic. After a flat section, you climb to the start of a 1.4 km downhill section that ends with an S-curve as the highway crosses the railroad just beyond the Soo River logging road. Shortly after, another steep grade leads to the start of a very long two-part downhill run. The first part is exposed and winding, and the second is straight with a left-hand turn at the bottom. Take the appropriate precautions and care. After cycling through more rolling country you climb up "Suicide Corner" to a viewpoint overlooking Nairn Falls (page 56). Take extra care on this steep ascent of just under a kilometre, because switchbacks are sharp and the shoulders limited. From a rest at the viewpoint, it is largely downhill to Pemberton. On a hot day you might want to stop at One Mile Lake (page 56), where you get your first view of Pemberton, for a cooling dip. In Pemberton you may wish to take the train back to Whistler to avoid cycling up the hills you have just come down. Check at the station for the exact time the train comes through, usually about 5:30 p.m.

If you arrive early enough you might continue up to D'Arcy, 44 km of severely rolling terrain away. As at Pemberton it possible to catch the train back to Whistler as it passes through, about 4:15 p.m., but check the times first in Pemberton or you will be cycling back not only to Pemberton but to Whistler as well. If you lack the time or are feeling lazy try cycling the flat, paved roads that go up the valley towards the farming community of Pemberton Meadows.

Easy cycling along logging road to nowhere

Callaghan Lake Logging Road (gravel)

Varied terrain and routes ... Waterfalls ... Lakes ...
Fishing ... Swimming

For variety and variations there are few rides better than the 30 km journey from Whistler to Callaghan Lake. From the Village you have the choice of cycling along the Valley Trail or Highway 99 to the south end of Whistler. These rejoin just south of the gondola. From here the route follows Highway 99 south to the Cheakamus Lake turnoff where you have another choice: either continue south along the highway, or take the Cheakamus Lake turnoff and wander along the logging roads until they rejoin Highway 99 near the Callaghan turnoff.

Cycle length: 60 km return
Elevation gain: Alexander Falls: 500 m
Callaghan Lake: 1080 m
Cycling time: 8 hours

Route: From Whistler Village head south to the Callaghan Lake turnoff (12.8 km on Highway 99). Turn right onto gravel road and follow it for 16 km to Callaghan Lake. Many variants on the main route are possible.

If you take the Cheakamus Lake option, do not take the left fork 800 m up the road (it goes to Cheakamus Lake), but head up to and through the Whistler garbage dump. On the far side of the dump, fork left uphill, then follow the road as it descends back to the valley, going right at any fork. Except for the 300 m through the garbage dump this is a pleasant and quiet route of 10.5 km that allows you to avoid Highway 99.

The road to Callaghan Lake branches off west of Highway 99, 200 m down from the very prominent basalt columns that both Highway 99 and the garbage dump route pass just before they join.

The gravel road is well graded and for the first 6 km is characterized by flat stretches joined by steep sections. At the 6 km mark there is a B.C.

Forest Service recreation site. Give yourself a break here by going the quarter kilometre down the side road to see alluring Alexander Falls.

Continue up the main road past the recreation site and across the Callaghan River. Just where it begins a steep climb, the road forks. The right fork goes to Madely Lake and the left one to Callaghan Lake. Although the 5 km journey to Madely Lake is steep and somewhat rough, it is well within the capabilities of the beginner and is well worth the effort.

The Callaghan fork climbs steeply for 4 km before levelling off and descending to the lake. Callaghan Lake is large and beautifully situated in a large bowl surrounded by snowcapped mountains. If you are a fisherperson and haven't brought your fishing rod, you will be kicking yourself, so don't forget it. On a very hot day you will find a quick dip in the cold water refreshing, but on a cooler day the swim is best forgotten. After you have retraced your tracks back to Highway 99, take some variations that you didn't do on the way out.

If you have the time and energy as you cycle back toward the Village, there are two alternate routes that will give you some additional enjoyment. The first is to turn right as you reach Highway 99 and cycle 5.4 km south to Brandywine Falls (page 46). Once here you can loop back along the Calcheak trail, which eventually meets Highway 99 half a kilometre from the Callaghan turnoff. Watch out for walkers. The second option is to take the Cheakamus Lake turnoff and cycle up to Cheakamus Lake (page 44). This route is 8.2 km long and involves 3.2 km of trail riding from the parking lot to the lake.

The Callaghan Lake tour makes for a solid but pleasurable day of cycling, especially if you do any of the side trips or spend time lazing about at any of the lakes.

Starvation Lake *(pavement and gravel)*

The best Whistler-to-Squamish route challenge yet available . . . Downhill . . . The last part is flat

A challenging ride from the Tantalus viewpoint into Squamish. This trip is ideal for intermediate riders and can be done by beginners, yet is not boring for experts. The difficult sections are short and can be quickly walked by the inexperienced rider.

Cycle length: 27 km one way
Elevation loss: 400 m
Cycling time: 3 hours

Driving distance from Whistler Village: 30.6 km

Route: Drive south along Highway 99 for 30.6 km from Whistler Village; park at the Tantalus viewpoint. Cycle 50 m up the highway (south) to an old powerline access road. Follow this road for about 8 km to the Cheakamus River, then another 3 km to a major bridge. After crossing the bridge, take flat roads on the valley floor to Garibaldi Highlands 16.0 km further on.

This is a great ride for beginners who want a challenging ride but don't want to stick their necks out too far. Yet this trip won't bore any experts who are along. When combined with the Callaghan Lake cycle and a stretch of highway riding, this is a great way to cycle from Whistler to Squamish as it minimizes the distance that has to be ridden on Highway 99 and limits it to one section of wide road. If at all possible, try to make this a one-way ride.

From the Tantalus viewpoint (page 134) in Cheakamus canyon go uphill for about 50 m to where an old road drops down to the right. The route follows this road all the way to the floor of the Cheakamus valley 8 km away. The road is very weathered, i.e., it consists of patches of loose gravel and rocks, an uneven surface and a few old rotting spans over minor watercourses. The first 4 km to Starvation Lake are characterized by a series of short, steep drops. You'll pass some edges that give good views of the river a couple of hundred metres below.

At the 4-km mark you will cross a stream that drains Starvation Lake, 100 m beyond. Just on the other side of the stream, a faint track runs out to a viewpoint. From here, you overlook the BCR tracks and the Cheakamus River below and see the distance you will be dropping in the next 4 km.

On the far side of Starvation Lake, the descent to the valley floor begins immediately and steeply. This drop is the first of two very steep and rough drops; the other is just above the valley floor. These drops, each a few hundred metres long, can be cycled by experts, but beginners should walk their bikes down these sections.

Once you are down to the valley floor beside the Cheakamus River, the rest of the trip is over gently rolling country on a quiet backwater of a road. It is 6 km to pavement in Garibaldi Highlands, a suburb of Squamish. When you reach the blacktop, it's a long but easy 5 km to Fergie's Resort (page 121). Here the traffic gets a little busier but is still considerably quieter than Highway 99.

If you do not have a ride back to the viewpoint you have two choices. Either retrace your steps; or continue 1.4 km along the road to the fork that heads to the Alice Lake turnoff on Highway 99, then cycle back to

the viewpoint along Highway 99. The former is more difficult but the latter is more dangerous because of the traffic and lack of shoulders.

The best alternative is to arrange for a pickup in Garibaldi Highlands or Squamish. Reach Squamish by going right at the intersection 1.4 km from Fergie's and staying on the main road as it winds its way along the valley floor and through Brackendale for nearly 7 km to Garibaldi Highlands.

If you are going to cycle all the way from Whistler Village, follow the Callaghan Lake route, taking the garbage dump variation to join Highway 99 at the basalt columns. From here, you can cycle 18.5 km along Highway 99 to the Tantalus viewpoint. Alternatively, cycle 800 m from the basalt columns to the Calcheak campsite turnoff and take the trail to Brandywine Falls and rejoin Highway 99 there, saving yourself 5 km of highway cycling. The Calcheak trail is slower but more challenging, while the highway is faster and shorter. Regardless of which option you choose, the highway between the basalt columns and the Tantalus viewpoint is wide with generally decent shoulders, making it as safe as highways get in this region.

Cross-Country Skiing

When the snow of winter hits the Whistler region, all the areas that provide magnificent off-road biking and spectacular hiking become winter wonderlands to be explored on skis. Although the trails at Lost Lake provide enjoyable skiing amid the mountain scenery, it is the off-track skiing that emphasizes the wilderness of the area.

Before venturing from the prepared trails, *be aware that you are going into the wilds in the winter and there is no room for error.* You must be well prepared. Although wandering off the prepared trails can be extremely serious business, if you start by following obvious routes that provide easy skiing, such as logging roads, you can have fun and enjoyment without endangering yourself or a rescue party. Most of the time you will be breaking your own trail. Although you might feel fresh, you will be considerably more tired than you feel and it will hit you suddenly somewhere on the return. It is better to turn around while you still feel chipper so that you make it back to your car before total exhaustion sets in. *Exhaustion and the related problems of hypothermia and bad judgment are the main causes of winter accidents in the Whistler area.*

If there is enough snow for you to ski then there is enough snow for avalanches. The best way to survive an avalanche is not to get caught in one. If you are going into the back country in winter, you should take an avalanche safety course and ski with experienced back-country skiers until you gain experience. Carry an avalanche beacon and know how to use it. Here are a few pointers for those who will be skiing on logging roads, or might due to circumstances beyond their control find themselves in avalanche country. *Avalanche country is best defined by saying if*

you can ski down it, it can slide. In general, the moderate slopes of 30–60° are the most dangerous. Gentler slopes seldom slide (but avalanches from above can sweep across them) and the steeper ones usually don't gather enough snow to create a major slide hazard. When checking terrain for its avalanche potential, study not only the terrain in your immediate area but also that far above you where an avalanche might start and below you to where you might be swept by a slide. Avalanches are capable of travelling extraordinary distances, whether it be from above to hit you or to carry you over some cliff far below. Stay out of gullies and little draws as they are the paths avalanches will follow. Swaths of alder and maple are other good indicators of avalanche paths; these are usually found in gullies. Two good rules that will keep you out of avalanche paths: stay on the higher immediate ground, and stick to areas with abundant tall, standing trees. In other words stay on the little ridges in the big timber.

If you must cross avalanche chutes, do so one at time and as quickly as possible with your avalanche beacons on. Those not crossing must have their shovels ready and their eyes on the person crossing. Avalanches are very difficult to predict. But, in general, the danger of avalanches is greater when fresh snow has fallen on a hard surface.

If you are caught in an avalanche there are four possible outcomes: you can be on the surface alive, or on the surface dead, or buried and alive, or buried and dead. If you are dead, then time is not a concern. If you are alive and on the surface, then time is a concern only if you need medical attention. If you are alive and buried, time is crucial no matter what your medical condition, because if you aren't found and dug out within 30 minutes your chance of survival is well under 50%. Remember, no amount of safety gear is going to help you if you are dead when the avalanche stops. This means the chance of surviving an avalanche in the back country, where by definition you are long way from help, is less than 25%. Given these odds it is easy to see why *staying out of an avalanche is the surest way to survive an avalanche.* And the surest way to stay out of an avalanche is to stay out of avalanche areas.

Snow in the wilderness is both enemy and friend. It's an enemy in that it forms avalanches that can kill and comes in storms that hide your tracks and route. But it is a friend because it can provide shelter and water. If you get lost or injured and have to spend a night out, dig a snow cave or bury yourself in the snow because snow provides insulation from the colder outside air. Even if you have a tent and stove, use snowbanks or walls as a screen to cut the wind chill down.

Frostbite is easy to get and easy to prevent. *Wind, wet, and cold surfaces, primarily metal, accelerate the onset of frostbite.* Most heat loss is from the head and neck. Dry toques, gloves, and socks go a long way to preventing frostbite in the extremities, where it occurs the easiest. Always take extras of those items. When your gloves and socks start to get damp take them off and put them against your stomach where your body heat will dry them if they are not too damp. At night take them into your sleeping bag. So wear wind proof clothing, don't get wet (this means sweat too), and avoid touching cold surfaces.

Snow reflects sunlight extremely well with two serious consequences that are often overlooked: sunburn and snowblindness. On a sunny day, and it does not have be very sunny, wear a good sunblock lotion. This should have a Sun Protection Factor (SPF) greater than 20. It not only prevents you from getting a sunburn but it stops the wind from drying out your skin. Remember to cover any skin that is exposed. For your lips, a lip conditioner of SPF 15 will do in most cases. Snowblindness is sunburn to the eyes. Sunglasses that block ultraviolet light are necessary, even in the fog and on overcast days. Expensive glasses aren't necessarily the best, and on a dull day even an ordinary pair of reading glasses will help. It is better to have proper glasses and preferably at least one spare pair per party. *Both frostbite and snowblindness are serious medical conditions that should not be underestimated. They contribute to many outdoor injuries in all seasons of the year, not just in winter.*

That's what happens when you grow up in Vancouver and climb the North Shore Mountains. You look north and climb those mountains, and you look north again. Well, it just never stops. If you become interested in the Coast Range, there's no cure for it.

John Clarke, 1989

Logging Roads

For a first off-track adventure you will do well to explore a logging road, as they are a beginning adventurer's dream. Roads are easy to follow, tend to avoid avalanche terrain, and there are lots of them. Are there good and bad ones? Of course! The ideal road is one that gives you access to a major valley and runs many kilometres back into nowhere without crossing avalanche paths. These roads are characterized by their great length over generally easy rolling terrain. As a rule avoid roads that climb the side hills unless you don't mind climbing steeply for a seeming long distance that seems considerably shorter on the way down. The side hills do, however, provide you with a very good and fast downhill run. These can be found branching off the road in any major valley and are a great way to start your return journey.

Two good, long roads near Whistler are the found in the **Soo River** and **Rutherford Creek** valleys. Both run back over 25 km from Highway 99. Both start by climbing steadily for the first 5 km before levelling off and running back toward the valley head. The Soo road starts 16.4 km north of Whistler Village 200 m before the road crosses the railroad tracks. The Rutherford is located 24.3 km north of the village, 200 m north of the bridge that crosses the river itself. The Rutherford is used by the Pemberton Snowmobile Club to gain access to the Pemberton Icecap and the Snekwnukwa7 Glacier (page 109). The club is a responsible group and although snowmobiles can be noisy, they provide an extra measure of safety, not to mention packing the deep powder down to make the skiing easier.

A little further afield and at a higher elevation, **Van Horlick** and **Blowdown creeks** at opposite ends of Duffey Lake provide easy wilderness skiing earlier and later in the season. Van Horlick is at the western end of Duffey Lake 34.8 km up the Duffey Lake road. From a fork 2.5 km up, roads run up both sides of the valley. Take the road on the east side for 10 km along the main valley before climbing steeply for 2 km to gain the north fork of Van Horlick. Blowdown Creek is located at the avalanche barrier about 4 km beyond the eastern end of Duffey Lake or 45.0 km up the Duffey Lake road. The road climbs steeply for 3 km before levelling off for 7 km, past which a steady climb of 8 km puts you on the Blowdown-Cottonwood pass looking down into the Stein valley.

If you want to do an overnight ski trip but do not want to camp outside, there are two popular trips within your reach. The **Elfin Lakes** cabin at Diamond Head (page 69) is an excellent venture to start with if you have never skied with a pack on your back. The ski to the cabin is easy, and many ski trips are available in the area. The shelters at the Battleship Islands in the Black Tusk area (page 73) and the Burton Hut across Garibaldi Lake at Sphinx Bay are popular with the ski-mountaineering crowd. The long climb up the Black Tusk trail and the ski down it with its sharp turns make wearing of skins and metal-edged skis highly recommended. The ski across Garibaldi Lake to the Sphinx cabin requires good wilderness skills, not because of the skiing, which after all is flat, but in case a storm moves in during the night and you have to :ecross the lake in the clouds.

Diamond Head

Snekwnukwa7 Glacier

Looking across the valley from the tops of Blackcomb and Whistler you can see nothing but mountains buried in vast icefields with glaciers descending into the valleys. What you are looking at is the beginning of a series of icefields that extend almost unbroken to Bella Coola, some 400 km to the northwest. This glacial complex, along with the Patagonian Icecap at the southern tip of South America, is one of the largest areas of ice in the temperate regions.

Trip length: 72 km return
Elevations: Start: 300 m
    Campsite: 2000 m
Trip time: 14 hours one way; overnight

Location: Pemberton Icefield, northwest of Whistler

Driving distance from Whistler Village: 24.5 km

Driving instructions: From Whistler Village, drive 24.5 km north on Highway 99 and turn up the gravel road coming in from the left. If snow conditions allow it is possible to drive up to the 26 km mark. The road switches to the south side at 19 km, just beyond the southwest branch of the Rutherford. Here, the logging road ascends the sidehill to the snowmobile cut.

 Climbing: Mostly easy ski ascents.

 Natural wonders: Glaciers, mountains, icefields.

Considering how close the Pemberton Icefield is to civilization, it is surprisingly difficult to reach without a helicopter. The Snekwnukwa7 Glacier with its good access via Rutherford Creek is probably the easiest and least complicated approach, yet this is only a recent development. Although lengthy in distance, the logging road is straightforward and steep only in the first 5 km and as you leave it to enter the woods. The road can be skied as a trip in itself if the snowline is low. Thanks to the Pemberton Snowmobile Club, a path exists through the woods and out onto the flat area below the glacier's snout.

The nice thing about the Pemberton Icefield and the glaciers descending off it is that there are few crevasse problems because of their gentle nature. This is not to say that they are not potentially dangerous, but they are about as safe as glaciers come. This factor and the relative lack of avalanche danger means they are ideal for beginners looking for their first backcountry and glacier experience. From the flat area at the glacier's snout a steep climb leads to the main, flat body of the glacier. Once here you can either ski up to the head of the glacier or climb the slopes on the south side. The slopes just beyond a rocky peak, called Syatsqua7 Skuza7, are ideal for practising your downhill technique. They have a variety of angles from which you can choose, according to your nerve and ability. The climb to the summit of Sam7am just above these slopes is easy and gives great views back into the Whistler area.

If you wondered how the features in this region acquired their unusual names with tongue-twisting spellings, it's because this particular glacier was first explored on skis by a group of Lil'wat Indian mountaineers, and they gave the features in the region names in the Lil'wat language. Snekwnukwa7, pronounced roughly Sho-new-qua, means family. The peaks around it bear the names of members of the family unit, such as Sam7am, pronounced Sh-mam, which means wife. The "7" represents a glottal pause similar to the one hears in the Cockney pronunciation of bottle, "bo'le."

Paddling

Although not prime paddling territory in terms of numbers of rivers and streams, there are nonetheless some classic paddles in the Whistler region for all levels of ability.

All the rivers and lakes in this area are snow-fed. The larger ones are glacier-fed and thus are cold, often extremely so. With that in mind, a wet suit is essential on all whitewater trips and is not a bad idea on any trip. You should also carry a change of clothes, well wrapped in at least one layer of plastic, and a thermos of hot liquid. A stove is even better. A towel, still another set of clothes, and another stove should be left in the car so that you will be dry and warm on the drive home.

Being mountain streams, the watercourses here tend to have steep rates of descent, rocky bottoms, and rapid changes in character. The water levels rise very quickly during extended periods of rain or hot weather, and the difficulty of a paddle can rapidly swing from one end of the paddling spectrum to the other.

Being mountain streams in a temperate rainforest, these rivers contain many sticks and stones, both seen and unseen, that can easily damage you and your boat. The narrowness of the streams and the size of the trees found here means that the trees can span, hang over, or lie in the water, creating a hazard that can have fatal consequences if you don't take care. Also, don't forget that log jams can create many unforeseen and dangerous problems. *For these reasons, helmets are essential to stop you from getting injured or knocked unconscious. A personal flotation device* (PFD) *or a lifejacket is mandatory and MUST BE WORN.* It does not do you any good if it is on one side of the river and you are on the other, and you can't put it on if you are unconscious.

While there are big lakes available to paddle, the funnelling effect of the mountains leads to winds that can whip up large waves on an otherwise calm day, making the water extremely dangerous. These big lakes tend to be wider than they look, making it is easy to get caught a long way from the shore. So get to shore, any shore, as quickly as possible if the wind picks up.

Photo by Robin Barley

Floatin' with a few friends on the River of Golden Dreams

River Of Golden Dreams

In Whistler... Unusual views... Slow moving water...
Peaceful marshes... Lakes

Located in the centre of Whistler, this trip gives you a chance to see the Whistler and Blackcomb ski areas from a different angle. The canoeing is on two lakes and a gently flowing connecting river. The river winds through the marshy area in the valley, giving entertaining but easy paddling.

River length: 9 km
Water: Slow, flat water
Boat: Canoe
Paddling time: 2– 3 hours

Location: Whistler
10 minute drive from Whistler Village

Driving distance from Whistler Village: 1.3 km on highway

Driving instructions: From Whistler Village, drive south on Highway 99 to either Wayside or Lakeside parks.
Put-ins: (1) Wayside Park, 3.3 km south of Whistler Village; (2) Lakeside Park, 2.8 km south of Whistler Village, is reached by turning right down Alta Vista Drive, continuing to the bottom, and bearing left to the end.
Take-out: Green Lake, along the shore beside Highway 99 north of Whistler Village.

 Hiking: Valley Trail.

 Camping: Campsites available at Calcheak (B.C. Forest Service) and Whistler Campground (commercial).

 Mountain biking: Unlimited amounts in the area.

Swimming: Lost Lake and Alta Lake.

 Natural wonders: Mountain scenery.

If you want to see Whistler from a different perspective and have a relaxing but entertaining paddle, try the River of Golden Dreams.

Put your canoe in at either Wayside or Lakeside parks on Alta Lake. Paddle northward to the end of the lake where the River of Golden Dreams leaves on its journey north to Green Lake. As you paddle the length of Alta Lake be sure to keep to one side of the lake; windsurfers use the centre of the lake because there is a constant wind funnelling down the Whistler valley.

Golden Dreams corkscrews through the marshy area between the two lakes, making a number of sharp changes in direction as it does. During high water, the flow will sweep you along, while at low water you might have to portage around a multitude of dead vegetation. Because of the narrowness of the river, many trees and bushes hang across and into the river, so paddle carefully.

There are a number of bridges crossing the river that you have to paddle under. The first is about 300 m down the river. The second group of structures, about 2 km farther down, comprises the Valley Trail bridge, followed by a sharp bend and the railroad tracks. The third and final group of bridges, just over 4 km downstream and just before the end, consists of an old wooden bridge followed in a few metres by the Highway 99 bridge.

If you wish, you can take out just before Highway 99 crosses the river, or finish on Green Lake at one of the many take-out points there. On Green Lake, you can turn right and get out near the floatplane dock. It's probably better to go left and take out at one of the viewpoints along Highway 99, at Green Lake Park (the spit of land halfway down the lake), or at the left-hand corner at the end by Highway 99.

Middle Lillooet River

Easy canoeing... Mountain scenery... Flat water... Wilderness stops... Paved road access... Stopping spots

A flat-water canoe trip on the fast-flowing Lillooet River, good for novices. Although you feel you are in the wilds while on the river, the good road access reminds you that you are never far from civilization. The views from the river of the surrounding mountains and icecaps range from breathtaking to majestic.

River length: 23 km
Water: Fast flowing, flat water
Boat: Canoe
Paddling time: 4 hours

Location: Upper Pemberton Valley
60 minute drive from Whistler Village

Driving distance from Whistler Village: 57.0 km on paved highway

Driving instructions: From Whistler Village, drive 31.9 km north on Highway 99 to the Pemberton junction.
Put-in: Turn left and drive up the Lillooet River road for 25.1 km to the bridge across the Lillooet River. The put-in is beside the bridge.
Take-out: Turn right and drive 2.1 km to the Lillooet River bridge. Take-out is on the right bank immediately upstream of the bridge.

Hiking: Pleasant strolling along the dikes by the take-out.

Camping: Campsites available at Nairn Falls just before Pemberton. Wilderness camping at many spots upstream of the put-in.

Mountain biking: The dikes offer easy mountain biking.

Swimming: At One Mile Lake just before Pemberton. The Lillooet River is unsafe for swimming because of frigid, fast-flowing water.

Natural wonders: Waterfalls, hanging valleys, glaciers, and mountain scenery.

If your canoeing experience is limited but you want to float through the mountains, then the Lillooet River is just what you ordered. The trip involves little more than letting your canoe float downstream on the wide river and some steering on the gentle bends. The canoeing problems are limited to two minor difficulties: the railroad bridge near Pemberton has the usual weird currents and eddies that are found near bridges; and because the river is diked care is required to avoid the sharp rocks when putting ashore.

Although this is a wide river with no whitewater, it is not to be treated lightly, as it is extremely fast-flowing and very powerful. Because it is glacier-fed, it tends to rise during times of high melt (May through July) on the glaciers, becoming even faster and more powerful, and is always very cold. If you are an inexperienced paddler, avoid this trip when the water is high.

As you float down the river you can see the effects that glaciers had on this area. The most obvious is the Pemberton Icecap, a remnant of the last ice age that you can just see spilling over the west side of the valley.

Although not as obvious at first, but unmistakable once you think about it, is a U-shaped valley you are in. A U-shaped valley is characterized by a flat bottom and steep sides, just like a U. The valley floor here is 2–5 km wide and the mountain summits are 2 km above the valley floor. During the last ice age a huge glacier flowed down this valley towards the Fraser Valley, scouring the sides of existing mountains.

While you float you will see two other types of valleys common in areas that were heavily glaciated. Hanging valleys were created where smaller and shallower side glaciers were truncated by the large trunk glacier that occupied the Lillooet valley. Hanging valleys are characterized by sudden steep drops at the end of gentle U-shaped valleys. They are frequently marked by a waterfall. The other common valley is a V-shaped one. Unlike the others they formed after the main glaciers receded, by water, not ice, carving a channel in the bedrock. The result is a valley that is only as wide as the watercourse with sides that lean back a constant angle. Usually these valleys lack spectacular waterfalls but have steep, fast-flowing creeks in them.

It is interesting to watch for these features as you paddle down the river. If you want to stop and admire the views over a sandwich, try the left-hand bank. It is quieter and there is a greater chance of seeing wildlife.

When you pass the railway bridge just before Pemberton, you are approaching the end of the trip. After paddling under some power lines, a left and then a sharp right turn signals the end. The Lillooet River bridge appears suddenly, and if you are not paying attention you will miss the best, but not the only, take out point near your vehicle.

SIAMESE TWINS..... JOINED AT THE CANOE.

Upper Lillooet River

Easy kayaking... Mountain vistas... Hotsprings... Easy road access... Wilderness setting

Starting near Meager Creek hotsprings, the first kilometre is rough water kayaking. But the rest is easy paddling with challenging route-finding through the meanders on a floodplain. The mountain landscape, wilderness setting, and easy kayaking make this a great trip for a novice kayaker.

River length: 35 km
Water: Fast flowing
Boat: Kayak
Paddling time: 8 hours

Location: Upper Pemberton Valley
2 hour drive from Whistler

Driving distance from Whistler Village: 92.1 km
57.0 km highway
35.1 km gravel road

Driving instructions: From Whistler Village, drive 31.9 km north on Highway 99 to the Pemberton junction.
Put-in: Turn left and drive up the Lillooet River road for 23.6 km to the intersection that leads to Meager Creek hotsprings. Turn right, go past the put-in for the middle Lillooet River trip at the bridge, and follow the road up the valley to the mile 24 marker, 60.2 km from Pemberton; turn left and drive to the bridge across the Lillooet. The put-in is at the bridge.
Take-out: Turn left and drive up the Lillooet River road for 25.1 km to the bridge across the Lillooet River. Take-out is just before the bridge. There is also a take-out at 22.0 km.

 Camping: Campsites available at Nairn Falls and Meager Creek hotsprings. Wilderness camping at various spots along the Lillooet River.

Mountain biking: Unlimited logging roads.

   Swimming: At One Mile Lake just before Pemberton; soaking at Meager Creek hotsprings.

   Natural wonders: Waterfalls, hanging valleys, glaciers, mountain scenery, and hotsprings.

The upper part of the Lillooet River offers novice kayakers a chance to improve their skills, particularly route finding, amid spectacular scenery. The trip is moderately challenging but fairly safe during low and intermediate water levels. It should be avoided during high water.

The put-in point is at the bridge that crosses the Lillooet on the final approach to Meager Creek hotsprings (page 138). The river at the put-in is swift, but a few hundred metres down the Meager joins it and together they sprawl over the Lillooet floodplain. Here the rate of flow and gradient ease. On the floodplain the river breaks up into an ever-changing series of channels. This type of terrain continues all the way down to your take-out point.

As you travel downstream, try and use broad channels with deep water. Avoid gravel bars and the usual assortment of tree problems, sweepers, and jams. Because this river is fed by fresh, ice-cold water from one of the larger icefields in the temperate world, wear a wet suit and take lots of warm liquids. Take time for a meal and snooze on a few of the many sandbars you come across.

If you are real crafty, you will take half the number of kayaks you need to accommodate the number of people in your party. Then, while half paddle down to the take-out at mile 14.4 (22.0 km), the others will drive the 7 km from the put-in to the hotsprings before going down to the take-out spot to pick them up (don't forget now). Then, after exchanging places, the first paddlers can return to the hotsprings, now 22 km away, before continuing down to the bridge and the take-out. If you want still more paddling, you can continue down the Lillooet to the Lillooet River bridge between Mount Currie and Pemberton (page 116).

Cheakamus River

Tree-lined banks... Rock gardens... Kayaking... Pools...
Small drops... 15 km from Squamish

A fast flowing river with rock gardens, small drops, and pools hidden among the trees 15 km north of Squamish. Here the intermediate paddler can run a whitewater river of medium difficulty in a wilderness setting.

River length: 12 km
Water: Fast flowing water
Boat: Kayak
Paddling time: 3 hours

Location: Squamish
    60 minute drive from Whistler

Driving distance from Whistler Village: 65 km
    60 km on highway
    5+ km on gravel road

Driving instructions: From Whistler Village, drive 47.0 km south on Highway 99 to the Alice Lake junction and turn left. Follow the signs to Cheekye and Fergie's Resort.
Put-in: Cross the bridge at Fergie's Resort and turn right. Go upstream and cross a second bridge. Go right, then across the railroad tracks, left and back across the tracks. There is a put-in at an island 2.1 km past the tracks. Another put-in is found by continuing upstream over a third bridge and 1.5 km to the end of the road.
Take-out: On the left side of the river at Fergie's Lodge.

 Camping: Campsites available at Alice Lake Provincial Park.

 Fishing: Good fishing for steelhead (catch-and-release) and salmon.

Swimming: Alice Lake.

 Natural wonders: Steelhead and salmon runs.

The Cheakamus River is good for the intermediate paddler who is just starting to paddle whitewater, as it provides a challenge in relative safety.

Turn west at the Alice Lake Provincial Park turnoff and follow the signs to Cheekye. The road crosses the river at Fergie's Lodge, and a right turn on the other side takes you upstream to the starting points.

When you're on the water, the trees on the river bank give you the feeling of being out in the middle of nowhere, yet the road is buried just a short distance past the trees. With a gravel bottom and a good volume, the inexperienced swift-water paddler has the chance to handle a rapidly moving boat without having to worry very much about ripping the bottom. However you will still have to pay attention to the trees that are likely to be either lying in the water or hanging over it.

There are two short class 3 drops on the river. The first is where Culliton Creek enters, and the second is beneath the bridge at the take-out. This first drop can be avoided by putting in at the first or "island" put-in 2.1 km past the second railroad crossing. If you want, you can skip the second drop by getting out before the bridge. When you climb out there is a cafe right at the bridge that not only has good food but also hot showers.

The Indians have their own names for the rivers and mountains of the Whistler region, and some of these names have found their way onto today's topographic maps. For example, "Cheakamus" is a Squamish Indian name meaning "a place where salmon traps are located." And the Squamish name for Mt. Garibaldi is "Cheekye," meaning "dirty place," which aptly reflects the appearance of summer snow on the mountain.

Birkenhead River

Rock gardens . . . Salmon run . . . Drops . . . Eddies . . . Wilderness setting

This short run for experienced kayakers is easily reached from Pemberton and has activities for the non-kayaker. In the fall, the salmon run provides an interesting natural spectacle. The river has a wide variety of challenges that can provide hours of entertainment.

River length: 5 km
Water: Fast flowing
Boat: Kayak
Paddling time: 3 hours

Location: Near Mount Currie
  60 minute drive from Whistler

Driving distance from Whistler Village: 44.9 km

Driving instructions: From Whistler Village, drive 31.9 km north on Highway 99 to the Pemberton junction.
  Put-in: Turn right and take the D'Arcy road for 13.0 km to the bridge across the Birkenhead River. Put in beside the bridge.
  Take-out: Turn right and follow the D'Arcy road for 7.2 km to the train tracks. Turn right onto a gravel road 20 m before the tracks. Follow the road for 1.5 km to a bridge and park on the far side. The take-out is just above the bridge.

 Hiking: Lillooet River dikes (p. 58) and Owl Lakes offer good hiking.

 Camping: Campsites available at Nairn Falls just before Pemberton, and at Owl Creek on the D'Arcy road between the put-in and take-out.

Mountain biking: The D'Arcy road offers great rolling rides on pavement.

 Fishing: Good fishing for trout.

 Swimming: At One Mile Lake just before Pemberton. The river pools on the Birkenhead are refreshing on a hot day.

 Natural wonders: Mountain scenery, salmon run.

The Birkenhead River has the look and feel of a true coastal mountain stream. Enclosed by trees, filled with boulders, and with the occasional gravel bar at its side, it drops at a steady rate. This is not a river for beginners, but is marvellous for good intermediate and better kayakers.

There are many spots along the road between Mount Currie and the Birkenhead bridge where you can see the nature of the Birkenhead. From the put-in point to the take-out the river is almost continuous rapids. These are very difficult in high water, with a couple of rock gardens. You will find lots of holes to play in and the waves can get well over half a metre high.

If you have non-paddlers with you, they can have a picnic at the B.C. Forest Service campsite at Owl Creek, 3.9 km from the railway crossing in Mount Currie. If they take the upper entrance and turn left after crossing the tracks they will be able to picnic at the river's edge and watch you go by. While you paddle they can swim in the river pools in the summer, or watch the spawning salmon in the fall.

When you have finished, your friends can pick you up and take you back to the warm fire they have made.

Fishing

Fishing near Whistler offers a quiet pleasure in the mountains. Although it is largely forgotten, the first resorts in the Whistler area were not ski lodges but fishing lodges. In fact, from the 1920s to the late 1950s, about 10 years before commercial skiing appeared in the Whistler area, this region, and the Whistler valley in particular, was the number one fishing destination west of the Rocky Mountains. It is tempting to think of Whistler's decline as a fishing centre as a result of overfishing and over-skiing but the real culprit was improved transportation. Until cars, good roads, and long vacations became common in the 1960s, the only way most people could have a fishing holiday was to take a train to an area where a fishing lodge was easily reached. And the shorter the train ride the better. Thus Whistler was perfectly situated. As these factors changed, so did Whistler's fortunes as a fishing centre.

For us, the important question is, "Is the fishing still as good as it was in its heyday?" The answer is a definite "maybe." Although there was some overfishing in days of yore, it was not as significant as the intrusions of modern man that have caused the fishing of yesteryear to go by the board. While the fishing ain't what it used to be, there is still much fine water left, especially for those who are willing to wander slightly off the beaten track.

Unlike hiking and canoeing routes, which can be described in detail, the description of where and how to catch fish cannot, if for no other reason than fish tend to move more frequently than mountains and rivers. In addition, most of the fun of fishing comes from the intellectual

Casting around for a quiet time

stimulation and challenge provided by the search, rather than the actual successful catch. How else can you explain the enjoyment fishermen get from hours of unsuccessful fishing?

Rivers and lakes in the Whistler area are primarily shore fishing areas. The difficulty of access and the small size of most lakes are the main reasons for fishing from the shore. The mountain lakes are accessible only on foot, which makes taking a boat in impractical. In addition, most lakes are small enough that you can cast across them, but even the lakes with road access are seldom boat fished. This is in large part due to the problems of trailing a boat through the mountains even on paved roads. The final straw for most boaters is the lack of boat launching sites for anything other than canoes. Boat rental systems have been discouraged by the high winds that unpredictably develop on the large lakes, making them dangerous for the unskilled.

The prime sport fish in this area are salmon, rainbow trout and Dolly Varden. These three dominate to the almost total exclusion of the many other types of fish found in this area.

The salmon of the Pacific Ocean are not a single species of fish but rather five. For the freshwater sports fisherman in this area, there is only one salmon species of interest, the coho. The coho is a 2–10 kg salmon with a torpedo-like shape. The fry spend a year in the stream before going to the ocean for two years. Taken as they leave the ocean they are strong fighters and extremely tasty. Although it is possible to catch them on a fly, most are taken using spinning gear with spoons and roe. They are most numerous from September to November.

As the other species of salmon in this area are illegal to catch because of extremely low stocks, I recommend that you have an experienced salmon fisherman along with you, and you practise catch-and-release fishing to conserve the supply of salmon.

Rainbow trout are the most important sport fish in B.C. and are widely used to stock lakes. Although they spend the first part of their life in streams and return there to spawn, rainbow are mainly lake fish. These fish reach 5 kg in large lakes in the region, but most of those caught, primarily in small lakes, are just under a kilogram. In general just about anything will catch you a rainbow, including that old standby, a worm.

The steelhead is an ocean-run cousin of the rainbow that spends the middle third of its life in the ocean where it grows rapidly to over 5 kg. Most steelhead spent two to four years in a stream before heading to the ocean. Those that return after two years weigh in a just under 5 kg, while those that remain there for three years will get well over 5 kg. There are two runs of steelhead, a winter run from November to May which spawn immediately. The other run is a late spring run in May and June. The steelhead in this region is a catch-and-release fish, which means you have to release any you catch. In order to do this properly, handle the fish gently and take the unbarbed single hook out as quickly and carefully as possible, then gently lower the fish into the water and let it go. You should do this with any fish you catch but aren't going to eat that night. The less you handle the fish, especially out of the water, the better.

Dolly Vardens are char and not trout as is commonly thought. Dollies are found most commonly in large lakes but are present also in small lakes and mountain streams. Dolly Varden that are river-run tend to be a shade of olive on top and silvery on the belly. The sides are characterized by spots of a reddish shade. They can weigh up to 10 kg but most are in the 2–4 kg range.

Fishing Holes

Here is quick overview the major lakes and rivers that are easily reached in the Whistler area. Most of the mountain lakes are stocked, usually with rainbow. Please check the fishing regulations before going fishing. Copies of the regulations are available in most sporting goods stores.

- **Alice Lake:** Good evening fishing for cutthroat and rainbows in the summer (page 49).

- **Alta Lake:** Large rainbow and some kokanee in the spring and fall on spinners. Located in Whistler.

- **Anderson Lake:** Trolling and fly fishing for Dolly Varden and rainbow in the summer months. D'Arcy is at its west end.

- **Birkenhead Lake:** Good fishing for medium rainbows in the spring and fall. Large Dolly Varden are also caught using lures. Located near D'Arcy.

- **Birkenhead River:** The river upstream of Mount Currie has good rainbow fishing in the spring and fall. Coho salmon are in the river in the fall. Dolly Varden are in the river all year.

- **Callaghan Lake:** Stocked with medium sized rainbow (page 97).

- **Cheakamus Lake:** Rainbows and Dollies on fly or spinners in the summer and early fall (page 44).

- **Cheakamus River** (page 121): The lower section of the river accessible from Cheekye, reached by turning west at the Alice Lake turnoff, has a steelhead (catch-and-release) run from Christmas to late May. Steelhead reach the Cheekye bridge about five hours after the high tide in Squamish. Coho and Dolly Varden are in the river in the fall. Lure fishing is best for all species. The mid-section of the river below the Daisy Lake dam just north of Rubble Creek and down to the canyon provides Dollies that take bait until mid-September. Good fly fishing for rainbow in September and October.

- **Green Lake:** Large rainbow and Dolly Varden using spinners or flies. Located at the north end of Whistler.

- **Lillooet Lake:** The best fishing occurs where river and creeks enter the lake. Good coho fishing in September. Dolly Varden are most numerous in the spring. The head of the lake is an Indian reserve on which fishing is not allowed. Situated south of Mount Currie.

- **Lillooet River:** Dollies and rainbows enter the river from the Fraser in April. Located in the Pemberton Valley.

- **River of Golden Dreams** (page 114): Medium rainbows on fly from spring to fall. Connects Alta and Green lakes in Whistler.

Pemberton and the Lillooet River from the top of Mt. Currie
Photo taken in 1974 by Glenn Woodsworth

Swimming Holes

**THE WATER IN THOSE ALPINE
LAKES IS CERTAINLY REFRESHING!!**

If you like swimming you will have no problem finding a place to swim in Whistler country, whether it be in a lake or river pool. There is one caveat, and it is a big one: the water in the Whistler area is largely snow- or glacier-melt and is definitely not warm.

To find the warmest water pick a small, shallow lake fed by snow-melt, and with a minimal in- and out-flow. The lakes are warmest late in the season after an extended hot spell. In general mountain tarns in the high alpine late in the summer provide the best swimming. Just about any trail that leads to the alpine will take you to an area that has a few tarns from which you can choose one you like.

Alta Lake in Whistler receives no glacier water and has three swimming areas: Wayside and Lakeside parks on the east side and the best, Rainbow Park, on the west. The water is relatively warm, but the winds often make swimming chilly.

For a family swim each town has one easily accessible lake with good swimming in water that is reasonably warm most of the summer. Alice Lake in Squamish (page 49), Lost Lake in Whistler (page 36), and One Mile Lake in Pemberton (page 56) provide good swimming and car access for family trips. Although not as warm as these, Birkenhead Lake in Birkenhead Lake Provincial Park is an ideal destination for a family out looking for swimming and boating. There is a boat launch and large grassy area abutting the swimming area. The lake bottom slopes gently so all ages can play in the water safely.

If you are looking for a mountain tarn to hike into and swim in, any trail described here will suffice to some degree. The best possibilities are in Lizzie Meadows (page 88), with Black Tusk (page 73) and Rainbow Lake (page 83) half a notch behind.

River pools are extremely cold and tend to have rocky bottoms. They are great for dips on very hot days. Extreme care is required when swimming in them as the currents outside of the pools are swift. The big valley lakes are usually too cold for anything but a quick dash in and out.

Photo courtesy of Western Canada Wilderness Committee

Odds and Ends

The activities in this section are a collection of singletons that don't really fit anywhere else. It's certainly debatable whether some of the items in this chapter are outdoor activities, but all take place outdoors in the Whistler region, and all provide experiences that are hard to find elsewhere. All are well worthwhile doing: try a few and see if you don't agree. They're wild and woolly but unbelievable. So as Monty Python would say, "And now for something completely different."

Tantalus Viewpoint

Cascading glaciers . . . Mountain spires . . . River canyons

A chance to view Mt. Tantalus and its glaciers without driving off the road. The views provide postcard photographs.

Location: Between Squamish and Whistler
30 minute drive from Whistler
90 minute drive from Vancouver

Driving distance from Whistler Village: 30.6 km

Driving instructions: From Whistler Village, drive 30.6 km south on Highway 99. The viewpoint is on the west side of the road. **Caution** is needed pulling out of the parking lot as the viewpoint is located on a very blind turn.

 Mountain biking: A good cycle from Whistler.

 Natural wonders: Mountain views and features.

When driving Highway 99 between Squamish and Whistler a cluster of ragged, heavily glaciated peaks dominates the view in Cheakamus Canyon. This group is called the Tantalus Range, after its highest peak. There are several pull-outs along the highway where you can stop and take pictures of this majestic scene. The best is about halfway up Cheakamus canyon, where there are a couple of picnic tables and a good view into the canyon as well.

The viewpoint is 26 km from Squamish and 30.6 km from Whistler. The turnoff is well marked if you are coming from Whistler, but if you are coming from Squamish the left turn into the parking lot is prohibited. No problem: just keep driving for a bit until you can turn around and approach the parking lot from the north.

If you look at the Tantalus Range you'll notice that this group is extremely rugged and craggy compared with the surrounding, rounded hills. During the last ice age, the glaciers acted like giant pot-scrubbers, scouring and rounding the tops and sides of the peaks they covered. Tantalus and its neighbours stood above the ice and escaped the scouring effect. You can see evidence of the scouring on rocks near the picnic tables. Look for glacial striations – parallel lines on the rock surface. These lines are scratches made by rocks and dirt that were pulled over the bedrock as the glaciers moved down the valley.

The Tantalus Range shows textbook examples of many features that probably showed up in a textbook in your school days. If you go down the left-hand skyline from the summit you are following an arête, while the skyline to the right is a ridge. If they look the same to you, it's because they are, except to climbers who use arête for a steep, sharp, craggy ridge.

In the notch between the two summits that form the main mountain mass is a sharp point of rock, or gendarme, named the Witch's Tooth. A gendarme is any smallish spike of rock on a mountain ridge. Lower down on the glacier that descends from the right side of the main peak is another spike of rock. This pinnacle is called a nunatak, an Inuit word for a feature completely surrounded by ice.

At the top of many of the glaciers just below the rocky peaks, you can see giant cracks in the ice, called bergschrunds, that seem to run along the boundary between the ice and rock. Bergschrunds form where the glacier ice pulls away from the snow and rocks above. These are the deepest, and for climbers the most dangerous, holes on the glacier, because they frequently have an inverted V-shape, which makes getting out difficult.

The glaciers fall steeply from the bergschrund to the valley below. As the angle of the slope steepens, the rate of flow of the ice increases. Here the glacier is severely broken by a jumble of crevasses called an icefall. Below the icefall there is a large area of light-coloured rock. The ice has just recently retreated from this area, and vegetation has not yet had time to become established. The retreat is happening because the amount of snow accumulating high on the glacier each year is less than the amount of ice melting lower down. These glaciers are receding at a rate of up to 30 m per year, making the retreat noticeable over a period as short as ten years.

When you pull back onto the highway be very careful, as you are coming out slightly uphill on a turn that is sharp and blind, especially for drivers coming from Whistler.

Hotsprings

Natural hotsprings . . . Wilderness surroundings . . . Winter access on skis

Hotsprings are common in western Canada, and the valley of the Lillooet River is blessed with several good ones. A hotspring is naturally hot water flowing out of the earth. In most cases the water is heated by circulating several kilometres into the earth, which is hotter than the surface. In areas of recent volcanic activity, such as Mt. Meager, a body of molten rock (magma) is located beneath the spring; water penetrates through the crack in the rocks and is heated by the cooling magma.

The water temperature depends partly on the amount of cold water mixing with the hot water, and changes over time. This change occurs over a matter of weeks, so make sure you check the temperature before you jump in any pool. Because the hot water makes you feel faint it is better to get out of the pool periodically to cool off, and go home a bit earlier rather than prolonging your stay to its maximum. How long you will want to stay in the pools will depend on the water temperature and to a certain degree on the air temperature, but as a rule of thumb twenty

The pools at Meager Creek

minutes at a time is plenty. Pregnant women, children and people with medical problems should check with their doctor before taking the plunge.

Harrison Hot Springs, the southernmost spring in the Lillooet River valley, has been developed as a tourist resort. From Vancouver, Harrison Hot Springs is a two hour drive on Highway 7 or Highway 1 and then Highway 9.

The three main undeveloped hotsprings in the Lillooet River valley can be reached by driving north from Whistler for 32 km to the northern terminus of Highway 99, a kilometre east of Pemberton. A right turn at this T-junction and another at the church in Mount Currie will put you on the road to the hotsprings at Skookumchuck and Sloquet Creek. A left turn will take you through Pemberton and up the valley towards Meager Creek hotsprings. Gas up in either Pemberton or Mount Currie as there are no services beyond the end of the paved road.

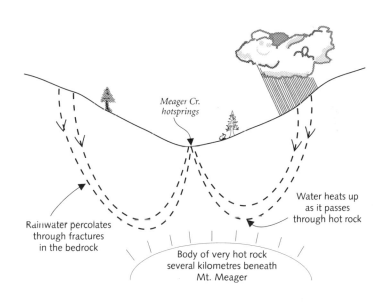

Cross-section through the Meager Creek area, showing how the hotsprings form

Meager Creek Hotsprings

Trail length: 500 m one way
Hiking time: 5 minutes

Location: Upper Pemberton Valley
2 hour drive from Whistler

Driving distance from Whistler Village: 100.2 km
57.0 km highway
43.2 km gravel road

Driving instructions: From Whistler Village, drive 31.9 km north on Highway 99 and turn left to Pemberton. Follow the upper Lillooet valley road for 23.6 km and turn right to a bridge over the Lillooet River. Cross the river and follow the main road as it runs up the river. Cross the river at mile 24 (60.2 km up and first left). Follow the road up Meager Creek for 8.1 km, going left at all the forks, to the parking lot.

Accommodation: B.C. Forest Service campsite with outhouses.

 Hiking: Logging road hiking only.

 Climbing: The Overseer and Manatee groups are accessible from here but are expeditionary country.

 Cross-country skiing: Only on logging roads, usually early or late in the season when the chances of getting snowed-in or avalanched-in is limited. Some avalanche hazard.

 Mountain biking: On logging roads, but watch for active logging.

 Swimming: Hot tub soaking.

Located at the edge of Meager Creek near the headwaters of the Lillooet River, the Meager Creek hotsprings are among the largest in B.C. They are also the easiest of the three Lillooet valley hotsprings to reach and the most visited. A good gravel road takes you to a huge parking lot near the pools. Ninety-five stairs and a short walk puts you on the terraces above Meager Creek, where warm streams, upwellings, and numerous pools border the Meager for about 400 m.

To reach the hotsprings drive north on Highway 99 to Pemberton. Turn left at the T-junction and drive up the valley for 23.6 km. Turn right at a conspicuous, marked intersection and follow the pavement to the bridge across the Lillooet River. Here the macadam ends. Continue up the gravel road, staying on the valley floor, until the mile 24 marker (60.2 km from Pemberton) where a road comes in from the left. This is the first major left fork past the Hurley Road turnoff at mile 6. Turn left and cross the Lillooet River a short distance later. Continue up the road, keeping left at all the forks, for 8.1 km to the parking lot.

Descend the stairs to the terrace, where a number of hot tubs and natural pools contain water ranging from the beautifully tepid to the very hot, allow you to sit and relax neck deep in the water. Camping is available in the area near the car.

In the winter the main Lillooet River road is frequently plowed to the Meager turnoff, and it is not unusual to find the road plowed to the last fork before the logging maintenance yard. You have to ski from wherever the plowed road ends. It is a pleasant experience, but remember you have to ski back to a cold car.

Stay out of this area during periods of heavy rain. The road is prone to washouts, particularly after the first heavy fall rains and in the spring. From June through September you can usually get your car to the hotsprings without trouble. At other times it's best to check with the B.C. Forest Service at Squamish (604-898-2100).

Skookumchuck Hotsprings

Trail length: 50 m one way
Hiking time: 1 minute

Location: Lower Lillooet River valley
2 1/2 hour drive from Whistler

Driving distance from Whistler Village: 94.7 km
38.5 km highway
56.2 km gravel road

Driving instructions: From Whistler Village, drive 31.9 km north on Highway 99 and turn right to Mount Currie. Drive 6.6 km and turn right at the church. Drive down the Duffey Lake road for 10.0 km and take the right fork that runs down Lillooet Lake. Follow this narrow gravel road for 46.1 km, where a road forks off to the right at power pole 68.2. This point is 6.6 km beyond Rogers Creek bridge, the only bridge the road crosses south of Lillooet Lake. Follow the road into the woods for 1.0 km and park.

Accommodation: B.C. Forest Service campsite with outhouses.

 Hiking: The Harrison-Lillooet trail (p. 144), Lizzie Meadows (p. 83).

 Cross-country skiing: Limited to logging roads in the area high on the mountain sides.

 Mountain biking: Logging roads but the area is actively logged.

 Swimming: Hot tub soaking.

 Historical wonders: Skookumchuck church (p. 147), Harrison-Lillooet trail.

Skookumchuck hotsprings are on the east side of the Lillooet River between Pemberton and the north end of Harrison Lake. Access is by the road running down the east side of the river. In the summer any car can make it to the hotsprings, but in winter you should carry chains.

The turnoff to the spring is 46.1 km down the Lillooet River east side road, or 6.6 km beyond the bridge across Rogers Creek, the first large creek past the south end of Lillooet Lake. At a power pole numbered 68.2, turn right on an old road that weaves its way to a dead end. The hotsprings are 50 m off to the left just below the main logging road. There are many nice spots for car camping near the springs.

The water here bubbles out of the ground and is piped into the tubs, actually parts of a septic tank. Because the water is extremely hot, cold water is also piped in. Check the water temperature before you get in, just in case someone pulled the cold water hose out and forgot to put it back in. The reverse can happen too!

This site tends to be overused and dirty, making it the least attractive hotspring in the area. Weekdays and winter offer your best bets for quiet and cleanliness.

So this is what a septic tank is for!   *Photo by John Clarke*

Sloquet Hotsprings

Trail length: 9 km return
Elevation gain: 125 m
Hiking time: 2 hours one way

Location: Lower Lillooet River valley
3 1/2 hour drive from Whistler

Driving distance from Whistler Village: 128.9 km
57.0 km highway
71.9 km gravel road

Driving instructions: From Whistler Village, drive 31.9 km north on
Highway 99 and turn right to Mount Currie. Drive 6.6 km and
turn right at the church. Drive down the Duffey Lake road for
10.0 km and take the right fork that runs down Lillooet Lake.
Follow this narrow gravel road for 29.0 km where a right fork
leads to the Tenas Lake bridge across the Lillooet River. Cross the
bridge and continue down the west side of the river for 51.4 km.
Here the road crosses Sloquet Creek. Don't cross the bridge, but
park off the road here. An old logging road starts up the north
side of Sloquet Creek just by the bridge. This is the start of the
walking.

Accommodation: Wilderness camping.

 Hiking: Logging road hiking only.

 Cross-country skiing: Limited to logging roads when the snow
is low.

 Mountain biking: Logging roads, but the area is being actively
logged.

 Swimming: Hot tub soaking.

Sloquet hotsprings are near the northern end of Harrison Lake. They can be reached by driving down the east side road to the Tenas Lake bridge, 29.0 km, and then the west side road for 51.4 km to the Sloquet bridge. Don't cross the bridge. Backtrack about 50 m to an old road and go 50 m up it and turn left up another old road. Park your car here as the road is very rough and the timeworn bridges are rotting. At the 5 km mark take the left fork and cross North Sloquet Creek. Depending on the water level you can either ford the creek or cross on the trees that are usually jammed across it.

In another hour, or 4 km more, you reach a steep down-grade, about 300 m long, which will take you to the hotsprings. There are a number of pools located among the trees, with the last and best being located right at the river's edge so you can hop back and forth between the hot and cold water for the maximum experience. The water is extremely hot where it emerges from the ground, but the pools are the temperature of a warm bath. After periods of high water the pools may be washed out. Feel free to rebuild them. In the winter when the snow is low this makes an enjoyable ski trip and is suitable for novices.

Hot pools by cold creek   *Photo by Glenn Woodsworth*

Harrison–Lillooet Gold Rush Trail

B.C. history . . . Gentle walking . . . Forest scenery

The prospector's original route to the Pemberton area and north to the gold fields of the Cariboo. The trail that remains makes for gentle walking, and the trip can be combined with other activities.

Length: 1–4 km return
Elevation gain: 0–100 m
Hiking time: 2 hours maximum

Location: Lower Lillooet River valley
2–3 hour drive from Whistler

Driving distance from Whistler Village: 81.8–125.3 km
38.5 km highway
43.3–86.8 km narrow gravel road

Driving instructions: From Whistler Village, drive 31.9 km north on Highway 99 and turn right to Mount Currie. Drive 6.6 km and turn right at the church. Drive down the Duffey Lake road for 10.0 km and take the right fork that runs down Lillooet Lake. Follow this narrow gravel road to any of the spots described below. Park and walk toward the river.

Accommodation: B.C. Forest Service campsites with outhouses.

 Hiking: The trail can be hiked. The longest section is about 4 km. Lizzie Meadows (p. 88) is nearby.

 Mountain biking: The road can be cycled from Pemberton.

 Swimming: Hot tub soaking at nearby Skookumchuck hotsprings.

 Historical wonders: Skookumchuck church.

To hike along the Harrison-Lillooet Gold Rush trail is to take a hike into B.C. history. This trail was developed during the gold rush that started in the late 1850s by miners eager to reach the gold fields. Because of the difficulties of travelling up the Fraser Canyon, the miners avoided it with a route that had been previously explored by the fur traders. This trail involved travelling by boat up Harrison Lake to Port Douglas, then trekking overland to Anderson Lake and continuing to Lillooet at the start of the Fraser Canyon.

During the first few years of the gold rush the trail was upgraded and roadhouses built. But when the road up the Fraser Canyon was finished in 1863, this longer route found itself out of business and within two years was abandoned.

Because of its relative isolation, much of the trail is still in existence. But with increasing use and development of the area, it is now threatened. Starting in 1977, Charles Hou and his students from Burnaby North Secondary School have done research on the trail and in the process have found many previously unrecognized traces of the old route. Each year they returned to hike the trail.

In 1989 the students arrived at Port Douglas to find that foundations of the early buildings and artifacts such as wagon wheels and sleighs had been destroyed by a mining company working a claim. We can't really blame the mining company: they didn't know they were destroying one of B.C.'s most important historic sites. The fault lies largely with the provincial government, which fails to protect such sites, often because it does not know about them and because they do not seem to have any economic importance. The remains of the trail should be protected by the creation of a narrow, linear park extending from Port Douglas to the south end of Tenas Lake and the trail cleared so visitors can hike it.

At present there are four places where the remains of this trail can be found easily. The northernmost is at the south end of Tenas Lake, where the outlines of 29 Mile House are still visible. Where the road forks 33.0 km from the Duffey Lake road, park your car and enter the woods below the power line. Two hundred metres down, on the edge of a bluff above the river, the road is obvious. Follow the road downhill (north) to the site of 29 Mile House, about 30 minutes from the car.

A second spot is located 500 m south of Rogers Creek bridge where a logging road meets the main road. Rogers Creek is the first major creek south of Lillooet Lake. Park here and hike towards the river, where you will intersect the trail just before the Lillooet River.

Another spot is 800 m south of Gowan Creek, the major creek 5 km south of the Skookumchuck church. Park your car at a pullout spot and

Skookumchuck church on the gold rush trail

walk into the woods for about five minutes until the land drops sharply down to the Lillooet river. The road is conspicuous at the edge of the drop. This section of road is about 2 km long and you are in the middle of it.

The fourth and longest section of trail is about 800 m north of the bridge that crosses the Lillooet River just before it enters Harrison Lake, or 9.0 km south of the fork to Port Douglas. A small spur road leads 50 m to the river bank. You can pick up traces of the road and follow it north for about 4 km. Initially the road is hard to follow as sections along the river bank have eroded away. Maybe someday the government will care enough to mark the trail better so you can hike a piece of history.

This trip can be combined with trips to Skookumchuck church (page 147) and Skookumchuck hotsprings (page 140) to make an enjoyable and varied outing.

Skookumchuck Church

Three gothic spires ... Stained glass ... Wilderness setting

This magnificent three-spired church from the turn of the century is the only large building in the Lillooet River valley below Mount Currie. The gothic beauty of the interior and exterior as well as its historical importance make the trip worthwhile. The nearby hotsprings and the Harrison-Lillooet trail make it more so.

Location: Lower Lillooet River valley
2 1/2 hour drive from Whistler

Driving distance from Whistler Village: 98.1 km
38.5 highway
59.6 km narrow gravel road

Driving instructions: From Whistler Village, drive 31.9 km north on Highway 99 and turn right to Mount Currie. Drive 6.6 km and turn right at the church. Drive down the Duffey Lake road for 10.0 km and take the right fork that runs down Lillooet Lake. Follow this narrow gravel road for 49.6 km, where a road forks right. The church is 300 m down the road.

Accommodation: B.C. Forest Service campsite with outhouses at Skookumchuck hotsprings.

 Swimming: Skookumchuk hotsprings (p. 140).

 Historical wonders. Harrison-Lillooet trail (p. 144).

This inspiring triple-spired wooden church is located in the village of Skookumchuck 4 km south of Skookumchuck hotsprings (page 140). Officially called the Church of the Holy Cross and recently restored to its original glory, this church is a must-see if you are in the area or have an interest in B.C. history.

The elegantly steepled church seems both to be an anomaly in the wilderness yet in harmony with it. Measuring 7.6 m by 21.3 m, it sits on huge, hand-hewn timbers. The interior of the church is one of the finest and most elaborate examples of pioneer carved decor in the province. Everything here is hand-carved. The ornate handiwork extends from one end of the church to the other and is painted in white and trimmed in gold. The stained glass windows give a fitting air and light to this magnificent building.

Europeans first started travelling regularly in southwestern B.C. in any numbers to reach the gold fields of the interior in the late 1850s. Because no easy route existed up the Fraser Canyon at the time, the miners reached Lillooet by following the Harrison and Lillooet river systems to Mount Currie and then to D'Arcy, where Anderson and Seton lakes gave easy access to Lillooet. This route remained in use until a road was built up the Fraser Canyon in 1863. With fortune-seekers travelling in droves up what was called the Harrison-Lillooet trail, religious organizations were not far behind. In this case it was the Roman Catholic missionaries who came along to "civilize" the native peoples.

Starting at the Scowlitz Reserve near Harrison Hot Springs several churches were built along the trail to the gold fields in Barkerville. Of the five churches originally built on the Harrison-Lillooet trail, those at Mount Currie and Lillooet no longer exist and those at Scowlitz and Seton Portage have been abandoned, leaving only the Skookumchuck church in use today. The present church, dating from 1906, is the third to have been built on this site; two earlier ones were destroyed by fire.

This church is well worth travelling the 4 km south of Skookumchuck hotsprings to see. In fact it alone is reason enough to bounce down the road for 72 km.

Duffey Lake–Hurley River Circuit

Mountain vistas . . . Climatic changes . . . Fishing holes . . .
Swimming lakes . . . Glaciers

This drive takes you across the Coast Mountains into the dry interior region of the province. In doing so it climbs up to the edge of the alpine zone and crawls along the edge of mountain canyons before reaching Lillooet. The return route threads through gentler territory before suddenly dropping back into the Pemberton Valley. The circuit covers many of the biogeoclimatic zones in the province.

Location: Between Whistler and Lillooet
7 hour round trip from Whistler

Driving distance from Whistler Village: 282 km (140 km highway, 142 km gravel road)
Pemberton to Lillooet: 95 km
Lillooet to Gold Bridge: 105 km
Gold Bridge to Pemberton: 82 km

Driving instructions: From Whistler Village, drive 31.9 km north on Highway 99 and follow the signs to Lillooet. Go through the town (not over the Fraser River) and follow the signs to Gold Bridge. Where a Bailey bridge leads into the village of Gold Bridge continue straight ahead for 200 m to another bridge that leads back to Pemberton.

Elevations:
Pemberton Valley: 200 m
Duffey Lake road high point: 1350 m
Lillooet: 265 m
Railroad Pass: 1450 m

Accommodation:
Hotels in Pemberton, Lillooet, and Gold Bridge.
B.C. Forest Service campsites along the route and on nearby side roads.

Hiking: Unlimited opportunities.

 Climbing: Joffre Group (p. 167) and many others.

 Cross-country skiing: Good skiing on the Duffey Lake and Hurley River sections but avalanche risk is high.

 Mountain biking: Unlimited side roads to wander up.

 Swimming: River pools exist along much of the route. The Hurley section near Gold Bridge has numerous good swimming lakes.

 Fishing: Good fishing along the entire route, especially along the Hurley and Gold Bridge roads.

 Natural wonders: Mountain features and great scenery everywhere.

If you want a breath-taking drive then here is one that is doubly breath-taking, the drive and the scenery. Although the route is straightforward, the driving is not. If you are not used to mountain roads and even if you are, be prepared; this drive is without a doubt a mountain one and the mountains rule the road. It is characterized by long steep hills, very sharp turns, and abrupt edges in both directions, frequently at the same point. Although large stretches of this route are now paved there is still much driving on gravel.

This is one of Canada's great mountain drives, encompassing most types of biogeoclimatic zones in B.C. The route makes a large loop from the northern terminus of Highway 99 near Pemberton through the towns of Mount Currie, Lillooet, and Gold Bridge before returning to Pemberton. Although it can be done in a day and as such is well worth doing, there are so many possibilities for side trips that you will enjoy it more if you take several days.

The journey starts by turning right at the T-junction at the northern terminus of Highway 99. The right turn to Lillooet at the church in Mount Currie is well marked. (Most of the whole tour is well marked, and where it is not, the important junctions are obvious.) After 10 km of level gravel through Indian land, the road begins to climb steeply – 1000 m in 14 km – before levelling out on its approach to Duffey Lake. This steep approach to the valley is necessary because the valley was created by a large glacier cutting off a smaller and shallower one as they merged without their bottoms meeting; the road climbs from the bottom of the deeper and larger valley to the smaller and shallower one. This smaller valley is called a hanging valley, because its end hangs above a larger one. The descent from Railroad Pass, at the other end of the trip, offers the same experience but it is steeper and longer.

Just before you reach Cayoosh Pass you will get a view of the glaciers and icefalls of the Joffre Mountain group. It is worth stopping here to stretch your legs and look at the magnificent views. Take the five minute walk from the Joffre Lakes parking lot to the lower lake (page 85) and savour the view. The B.C. Forest Service campsite here is the first of many on this circuit. Although you won't want to stop at all of them, do stop at a few to give yourself a break and take in the fresh air.

The road now winds its way through the mountains to Lillooet. The glaciers disappear as the climate becomes drier. Glaciers need the large amounts of snow that are dumped on the western side of the mountains; here there just isn't enough winter snowfall to support glaciers. There are numerous places to stop and take in the views. One place of special note is the boat launching site at the east end of Duffey Lake, the large lake you drive along, as it gives a fine view back into the Joffre group. Another good spot is 3.9 km further east at a barrier where a road doubles back into Blowdown Creek. This road gives you access to the great hiking in the alpine area above the Stein valley, but if you want to do this side trip you will require at least two days to drive this circuit.

Lillooet was Mile "0" of the Cariboo Trail in the gold rush days of the late 1850s. From Lillooet, the trail ran up the Fraser and inland to 100 Mile House, Williams Lake, and finally Barkerville. The bridge that crosses the Fraser here is called the "Bridge of 23 Camels." It was named for the 23 camels that were imported to carry supplies up to the gold fields in the gold rush days. This venture failed, because the camels smelled, were difficult to handle, and drove the horses crazy.

Drive through Lillooet and up the Bridge River towards Gold Bridge. This area is in a dry climatic zone, as you can tell by the red-barked Ponderosa pine and grey-green sagebrush. At the 10 km mark, just before you cross the Bridge River and leave the pavement, you can see the rocks along the Fraser from which natives fish for salmon in late summer. From here the road follows a narrow river valley with many abrupt edges. At one point, 39 km from Lillooet, a cliff overhangs the road. After 50 km, you reach the dam that holds back Carpenter Lake.

If you have time, you might make a side trip to Seton Portage and Shalalth. These two villages sit on the land between Seton and Anderson lakes. You saw Seton Lake as you descended the Duffey Lake road into Lillooet, and Anderson Lake is at the end of the paved road you turned off from in Mount Currie. There is good swimming in both lakes. The drive, which is 25 km long, starts by going across the dam, through a tunnel and along the lake before climbing up and over Mission Pass. Although the road is wide and in good condition, the drive is a hair-raising challenge as it is extremely steep and long. Gear down and enjoy the thrill. Just remember you have to return unless you have a rugged enough car to take the powerline route through to D'Arcy and Mount Currie. This is a narrow, extremely winding and rough road with many absurdly steep but short sections.

From the Carpenter Lake dam, the road follows the lake until you are 10 km from Gold Bridge. The road is winding but level and in good shape. Eighty kilometres of gravel road from Lillooet, you reach the final 10 km of pavement that leads to Gold Bridge. At the start of the pavement, a side road heads up to Tyax Mountain Lake Lodge. This 10 km side trip is well worth taking, as the lodge has a magnificent location and presents an opportunity to stretch your legs and enjoy a posh lunch.

The drive from Lillooet to Gold Bridge is marked by a relative scarcity of trees. Here the dryness of the climate and the poor soil cover limit tree growth. The area is dominated by the Ponderosa pine, whose cones have an interesting ecological adaptation. Their scales are tightly shut and in order for the seeds to be dispersed the scales must open. This they only do when they are exposed to temperatures of more than 45° C. As a rule it takes the heat of a forest fire to open the scales and allow the seeds to be released. This adaptation allows the seeds to remain dormant until the existing trees have been burnt, preventing an overuse of the limited amounts of soil and water. It also allows them to be the first trees to reseed after a forest fire. The tightness of the scales severely limits their use by squirrels and other rodents. As you approach Gold Bridge the vegetation cover starts to get back to "normal."

Just before Gold Bridge watch for a steel bridge that will take you into the town. Two hundred metres past the bridge, the road back to Pemberton turns off to the left and up the Hurley River road. If you drive through the town of Gold Bridge the road continues to Bralorne, a picturesque town 11 km away. Gold Bridge and Bralorne are old mining towns. Until the 1970s, mining was the main industry here, and the area is still heavily prospected today. In Bralorne you have the option of returning to Gold Bridge or taking a logging road until it rejoins the Hurley River road at the B.C. Forest Service campsite of that name.

Before starting on the return road to Pemberton, you might consider continuing up to Gun Lake, where two B.C. Forest Service campsites give access to the lake for swimming and boating. These sites are 7 and 10 km from Gold Bridge.

The Hurley River road from Gold Bridge to Pemberton begins by climbing steeply for a few kilometres before levelling off somewhat. The route is easy to follow as it climbs to Railroad Pass through country that even by local standards is majestic. The descent from Railroad Pass to the Lillooet valley and Pemberton is initially gentle, but where the new and old roads split things change. The left fork is the old unmaintained road. The right fork, the new road, takes you to the other side of the narrow valley before descending at an ever-increasing angle. Just a thought: the old road is even steeper and when it was maintained it was rougher, too. About 5 km down this section, pull off to the side and look at the views across the valley and at the drop into it. At the bottom of the hill, the road merges into the upper Lillooet River road. If you turn right (up-river), forty-five minutes will put you at the Meager Creek hotsprings (page 138). A downriver direction and 8 km will return you to the pavement and shortly thereafter to Pemberton. As you head down the valley, Mt. Currie dominates the view from your front window as you finally get an opportunity to relax.

British Columbia Railway

Train ride... Lake edges... Quiet mountain valleys... Rushing creeks... Mile "0"... Dry interior climate

A lovely day return trip to Lillooet that travels along mountain streams and lakes. Crossing the Coast Mountains you go from a wet climate to semi-desert. The trip can be done from either Whistler or Vancouver.

Location: From Whistler to Lillooet and back again
10 minute drive from Whistler

Driving distance from Whistler Village: 4.6 km

Driving instructions: From Whistler Village, drive 3.9 km south on Highway 99 to Whistler Creek (Gondola). Turn right at the Husky station and drive to the end of the road. Turn left and stop at the sign for the train station.

 Hiking: Walking around the town of Lillooet.

 Mountain biking: Mountain bikers frequently catch the train back from points to the north.

 Natural wonders: Different biogeoclimatic zones.

If you want to see the great changes in scenery and climate across the Coast Mountains but you have neither the means nor desire to drive the mountain roads to Lillooet, then consider the train that runs daily from Vancouver to Whistler to Lillooet. And back.

The BCR was until 1976 called the Pacific Great Eastern or PGE for goodness knows what reason. Construction of the railroad, which was intended to go from Vancouver to Prince George, started in 1912 but was not competed until 1956. The laying of the tracks was somewhat strange, to say the least, as it seemed to consist of laying a stretch of tracks that went from the middle of nowhere to the middle of nowhere. There were a series of these sections spread across the planned route and they were extended whenever there was money to buy another tie or two.

In 1907 a private company, the Howe Sound and Northern Railway, start to build a rail line out of Squamish, but after only 16 km it went bankrupt. In 1912 the PGE took over the project and by 1916 had extended the track to Clinton. By 1921 the railway extended to the Cottonwood River north of Quesnel and tracks led south from Prince George. At this time the politicians decided the cost of crossing the Cottonwood River was too much and, with less than 80 km to go, construction was

Photo courtesy of B.C. Rail

stopped. Quonset became the temporary northern terminus for the next thirty years.

South of Squamish the situation was similar. The line from North Vancouver to Horseshoe Bay was completed and opened in 1914. That done, things ground to a halt. This section operated until 1928, when it was abandoned until the Horseshoe Bay to Squamish section was completed in 1956. During the intervening years, the residents whose backyards faced the line used it to enlarge their gardens. This use of the line somehow fitted in with the demeanour of the whole operation, as train crews often stopped to pick berries. The nickname "Please Go Easy" was well earned.

Upon completion of the line, things became more efficient as the railway soon became a major transportation route for goods from the northern interior. The passenger train using cars made by the Budd company, called "Budd Cars," had for years taken people from Squamish, where they arrived by boat, to Lillooet and other interior destinations. Nowadays the train leaves North Vancouver at 7:00 a.m. daily and arrives at Lillooet at 12:30 p.m. Three days a week, half the train continues up to Prince George for an evening arrival while the other does what the train always does at 3:00 p.m. – returns to Vancouver.

The Whistler station is located behind the Husky station in the Whistler Creek area and is the reason that the original ski lifts were built here in 1965. At that time, the only way for most people to reach the area was by train. The road north from Squamish had just opened and was a narrow paved two-laned affair that makes today's road look prairie-straight. As the train pulls out from the station at 9:30 a.m., it weaves along the eastern side of Nina and Alta lakes giving you views of Blackcomb and Whistler mountains. At the northern end of Alta Lake it crosses the River of Golden Dreams to the west side of Green Lake, in which Rainbow Mountain is reflected on sunny days. From here the line makes a steady 30 km descent to the Pemberton Valley, largely along the banks of the Green River. Just before Pemberton the train crawls along the edge of the canyon above Nairn Falls.

Just beyond Nairn Falls the line enters the Pemberton Valley. One of the first white settlers here called this valley "the largest corral God ever built." This is a very accurate metaphor, as the valley is encircled on three sides by mountains that exceed 3000 m and blocked on the other by a valley-wide lake that is 20 km long. The valley has over 8000 hectares of prime agricultural land that is famous around the continent for the seed potatoes it produces. These are grown here because the valley is isolated from other areas, thus allowing the development of pure strains of potatoes that are unaffected by disease.

After Pemberton the train rolls through Mount Currie before turning up the Birkenhead River to D'Arcy. The Birkenhead in September is full of spawning salmon. The further up the valley the train gets the drier and drier the landscape becomes, as mountains closer to coast have taken most of the rain out of the clouds. From D'Arcy to Lillooet the drying trend continues as you twist and turn your way along the edge of first Anderson Lake then Seton Lake. These are typical mountain lakes in that they are long and fill the entire width of the valley. The slopes are very steep, not only above the tracks but continuing down below into the lakes themselves. These mountain lakes are characterized by incredible depths. When you combine these two factors and throw in the large amounts of loose rock, the potential for a disaster is clear. In fact more than one train sits in the depths of the lakes, the result of rockfall causing derailment. And finding the trains is difficult and on occasion impossible because of the depth of these lakes. Don't worry, because the railway runs speeders in front of the train to check for rock on the tracks.

Upon arriving in Lillooet at lunch time you will have a couple of hours to explore the town that at one time in the 1860s had 15 000 people in it, most of them heading up the Cariboo trail to the gold fields in Barkerville. When the train leaves at 3:00 the high school students who live in Seton Portage will be on it returning home after attending school in Lillooet. A special train takes them to Lillooet in the morning. Your train arrives in D'Arcy at 4:30, Pemberton at 5:15, and Whistler at 6:00, just in time for you to go out for dinner.

Murphy in the Outdoors

If you pack it you won't need it; if you don't you will.

The item you want is at the bottom of your pack .

If you unpack your pack you'll never be able to repack it as neatly or reduce it to the same volume again.

Taseko Lakes Plane Tour

Flying... Icecaps... Mountain valleys... Lakes... Glaciers

This figure-8 loop takes you across the Coast Mountains and over the Chilcotin Plateau. You begin by flying up the Whistler and Pemberton valleys, then skirt the edge of huge icefields before reaching Taseko Lakes. On the return, you follow the interior edge of the Coast Mountains and cross the Pemberton Icecap to Whistler.

Flight length: 250 km
Flying time: 90 minutes

Location: Green Lake, Whistler
10 minute drive from Whistler Village

Driving distance from Whistler Village: 4 km
3.2 km highway
0.8 km narrow gravel road

Driving instructions: From Whistler Village, drive 3.0 km north on Highway 99 and turn right. Follow the road to the end and turn left on a gravel road. Drive to its end at Green Lake and the floatplane dock.

 Natural wonders: Glaciers, icefields, mountain scenery.

If you can afford to spend some money, here is a great way to see a lot of fascinating country from a different angle – from the air. The trip will cost about $600, or about $125 per person if you have 5 people in your party.

The flight starts with a take-off from Green Lake, and depending on wind conditions a loop over Whistler itself at the beginning or end of the flight. You proceed up the Whistler valley towards Pemberton. As you approach Pemberton, the plane will do a left turn around Mt. Ipsoot and over Goat Meadows to gain the southern edge of the Pemberton Valley. On your left as you fly up the valley is the Pemberton Icecap, one of the smaller ones in this area(!) while a thousand metres below is the Lillooet River. About ten minutes up the valley you will see the trident peak of Meager Mountain, beneath which are the Meager Creek hotsprings.

If you look down to the Lillooet River below Mt. Meager, you can see the river shooting out of a narrow gorge into space. The waterfall is called "The Teaspout" (page 14) for the obvious reason. This gorge is the result of the Lillooet River cutting down through the ash left by a volcanic explosion near Mt. Meager some 2400 years ago. Ash from this eruption has been found as far east as Edmonton.

Just before you reach the glaciers at the head of the Lillooet valley you turn up Salal Creek and go over to the head of the Bridge River, then down Lord River valley to Taseko Lakes. Here you are flying along the southern edge of one of three vast expanses of ice that together extend almost to Bella Coola, 350 km away. In this land it is possible to walk for two weeks without setting foot on vegetated land. As you cross the toe of the Bridge Glacier, notice its width and length. If you are lucky, the lake at its toe might contain icebergs; some over 2 hectares in size have been spotted. When you enter the Lord River valley, look out the right window at the Downton Range and its alpine meadows that are interspersed with small glaciers.

Coffee break on Taseko Lakes

After a loop over Taseko Lakes, the plane will head up the Taseko valley and over the fabulous hiking country of Warner Pass (page 189) before reaching the town of Gold Bridge. Here you are on the edge of the Chilcotin Plateau and the views are stunning. The question is, do you keep your nose pressed against the window or shoot a whole roll of film? At Gold Bridge, the pilot will head southwest towards Whistler. You fly up the Hurley River to Railroad Pass. As you cross Railroad Pass the ground suddenly seems to disappear beneath you as you look straight down into the Pemberton Valley.

If conditions are right, rather than retracing the first part of your flight, the pilot will take you over the Pemberton Icecap for an unbelievable finish to a great trip.

Pack a sandwich and a thermos of coffee, and you might be able to talk the pilot into landing at Taseko Lakes for a quick lunch on the beach. Or just offer to buy him a coffee at Tyax Mountain Lake Resort on Tyaughton Lake.

Murphy in the Outdoors

The downhill journey has more uphills than the uphill journey has downhills.

The second half of a trip is longer than the first half. The amount of ascent is always more than the amount of descent.

"Just around the corner," "One more bump," and "We're almost there" when translated mean "You are nowhere close to your destination."

Wheelchairs

This section lists trips that have reasonable access for those who require a wheelchair for any degree of mobility, with an indication as to the difficulties a wheelchair operator might face. For further information consult the indicated page.

Campsites *(pages 29–32)*

- **B.C. Forest Service campsites:** These are little more than cleared areas with water nearby, picnic tables, and an outhouse with no allowance for wheelchairs.

- **Provincial Parks:** The provincial parks vary in their wheelchair accessibility. Alice Lake and Birkenhead have the best facilities, i.e., washroom and changing facilities. Considering that these parks are provincially owned, there is no excuse for not upgrading the facilities in the near future.

Short Trips *(pages 35–63)*

Not long ago, these trips would have been considered the only appropriate outdoor excursions for those in wheelchairs. These trips are short (in general less than a kilometre), travel good terrain (pavement or smooth packed terra firma), and most do not require assistance.

- **Shannon Falls:** Easy and short but uphill.

- **Alice Lake:** The trail around Alice Lake is flat and well-packed fine gravel.

- **Brandywine Falls:** Good path, but awkward crossings of the railroad and three steps up to the viewpoint.

- **Skookumchuck hotsprings** (page 140): Drive to within 50 m, good trail to the tubs, and excellent access to the tub.

- **Joffre Lakes** (page 85): A narrow dirt trail to the lower lake.

- **Lillooet Lake walks:** Limited access along the beaches.

- **Lillooet River dikes:** A flat, roughish dike-top road. Getting past the gate is awkward.

- **Lost Lake:** Easy access to the swimming area and surrounding trails.

- **One Mile Lake:** Good trail around the lake but the access to boardwalks is a pain (one step).

Long Trips

These journeys are longer and more challenging than those above. Fitness and sturdy wheelchair wheels will go a great distance to making the trips more enjoyable. All said and done, these are within the capabilities of many wheelchair-bound people, especially if a friend is along to help on the short sections, such as mud holes and smooth rock, that might otherwise prevent further progress. If you are short of strength and/or experience you may need an occasional push from a friend.

- **Alpine Whistler:** The Whistler Express Gondola is designed to be wheelchair accessible. From the top of the lift there is a good trail to Harmony Lake. Whistler has recently upgraded its wheelchair facilities; ask at the bottom of the lifts.

Rollin' in the gloamin'

- **Valley Trail** (page 93): Undulating mixture of gravel and pavement with access from a variety of points including Whistler Village and Rainbow Beach. A great route for views and exercise.

- **Cheakamus Lake** (page 44): After a very awkward drop from the parking lot, an old road and undulating terrain give access to the lake. The first hill is rough and long but the travel is better and more enjoyable in the woods.

- **Cougar Mountain** (page 41): The amount of logging road travel depends on where you park your car. The further up the less the distance and the fewer the hills. The climb out of the bowl and into the forest is steep but short, after which the path is essentially flat.

- **Lost Lake trails** (page 36): These run around the lake and can be reached directly from Whistler Village. Good surfaces on camel's back terrain.

- **Nairn Falls** (page 56): Gentle and undulating until 100 m from the falls where it turns to rock slabs on which assistance will be needed.

Swimming Holes (pages 131–132)

- **Alice Lake:** Good access, and changing facilities for the handicapped.

- **Lost Lake:** Good access to swimming area, no changing facilities.

- **One Mile Lake:** Good access to swimming area, no changing facilities.

- **Birkenhead Lake:** Good access to swimming area, changing facilities.

- **Alta Lake:** Rainbow Beach has good wheelchair paths.

Paddling (pages 111–124)

Access to and from the water might be difficult but only for a very limited distance. Given a bit of forethought and a reconnaissance, there should be no problem with paddling.

Fishing Holes (pages 125–129)

The lakes you can reach by car have some place where you can reach the shoreline in a wheelchair. Access to the rivers is variable and many will require patience to find a good approach.

Odds and Ends (pages 133–160)

- **Skookumchuck church:** Two steps into the church, but it's in a village so assistance can be found if you fail to bring your own.

- **Tantalus viewpoint:** If you are lazy turn your car so you can see the view without getting out.

- **B.C. Railway:** A wheelchair lift is located in North Vancouver. The rumours are that other large communities will be getting them but don't hold your breath, especially at the small communities, and forget it at the flag stops. Another major problem is that there are four narrow steps between the door and the ground. B.C. Rail will provide you with a narrow wheelchair for movement within the train.

- **Taseko flight:** No lifts here but that is a problem with the size of the aircraft rather anything else. Good access to the side of the plane where a human lift can easily be rigged. If movement is required within the craft it will be awkward but it is for everyone because of the small interior.

Adventures

These are for the very fit using strong wheelchairs. As they involve substantial changes in elevation, the ability to push uphill is required as is the ability to descend in control. A strong wheelchair with mountain-bike tires will make the journey much more enjoyable.

- **Logging Roads:** If you can find an unused road you can find a way into the remoter reaches of the area. Be prepared for some challenges including rough surfaces and stream fording, and adventure.

- **Meager Creek hotsprings** (page 138): 95 stairs down so say no more. This is too bad, because it is such a short distance. The old way that starts near the bend just below the parking lot offers more hope as it has less downhill but is a bit more rugged and still has 30 stairs.

- **Van Horlick Creek:** A flat smooth road off Duffey Lake that leads back towards the north fork of the Stein.

- **Blowdown Creek:** Drive to the 10 km mark. Steep initially but gives access to the alpine above the Stein. An alpine lake can be reached with a bit of 4x4ing. Worth the effort.

- **Sloquet hotsprings** (page 142): A potential classic for the fit athlete. The first kilometre is a washed-out logging road and uphill but can be done if care is taken. The next 4 km are flat and for the most part good going. There are a number of rivulets that have to be crossed but it's part of the fun. The crossing of the North Sloquet Creek is serious business. It is less than 10 m wide but seldom gets less than 50 cm deep. It is best to cross it in a 4x4 vehicle, or get carried across. The road on the other side is in good condition and flat until near the end where it climbs steadily to the top of a hill. As the last part is 200 m of steep rugged downhill, it is probably a good idea to get someone to help you with the descent as there are no runaway lanes. The best pools are 50 m into the woods and not wheelchair accessible, but if you made it this far I'm sure you will find a way. After a swim, a winch or some friends who do not mind pushing will be needed to get the chair up the first hill. Then return to the car by the same route. Drive home via the hotsprings at Skookumchuck, which are definitely more wheelchair accessible, so everyone can loosen up again.

Mountaineering
& Rock Climbing

Mountains in the Whistler region offer many fine climbs, from easy to difficult and short to long. Because it is not a climbing guide, this section does nothing more than indicate some areas that are worth investigating because they contain good concentrations of nice climbs. Bruce Fairley's *A Hiking and Climbing Guide to Southwestern B.C.* (see Helpful Books) provides the details you need if you are going to climb in the Whistler region.

For rock climbers, the walls, slabs, and short cliffs near Squamish offer some of the finest climbing in North America, on superb granite.

Although by local standards this is a heavily travelled area, it isn't by the standards of European and many other North American areas. Probably well over half the surrounding area is visited by mountaineers less than once a decade. Although almost all the peaks have been climbed at least once, many good new routes remain to be done. In general, climbers have concentrated on the western boundary of Garibaldi Park and the Joffre Lakes area.

The region may be broken down into three general areas. The popular **Garibaldi Park** area, between the Cheakamus and Lillooet rivers and north of Squamish, has good access on the western side and poor access elsewhere. It contains glaciers and small icefields, rock that is so-so at best, and many deep valleys. The **Pemberton Icefield** area, enclosed by the Squamish, Cheakamus, and Lillooet rivers, is a southern cousin to the huge icefields found further northwest. The extensive glacier systems are not broken by icefalls and give easy travelling and climbing; the rock varies from very good to very bad. It is popular with the ski-mountaineering crowd because of the terrain's gentle nature. Access is a problem but is improving. The interior ridges east of the Pemberton Valley in general provide mountain scrambling rather than mountain climbing. The **Joffre Group** is an important and popular exception, on loose rock in an area of limited glaciation. Access to this area varies from very good to difficult.

The more popular climbing areas, from south to north, are:

- **Mt. Garibaldi:** Access is from Diamond Head (page 69) and is very good. The rock is lousy and the routes stay on the glaciers. This mountain would be ignored except that it is so obvious and spectacular when seen from Squamish. The west side of the mountain offers some exciting and challenging winter climbing.

- **Black Tusk area:** Access is by the Black Tusk trail (page 73). The Tusk itself is a popular scramble although the rock is loose. The best climbing is on the far side of Garibaldi Lake. Access is easiest in the spring when you can ski across the lake, and the glaciers and reasonable rock provide enjoyable climbing.

- **Singing Pass:** Approach via the Singing Pass trail (page 77). The peaks here provide pleasant mountain scrambling to spectacular viewpoints. Although technically easy, they should not be underestimated because of the glacier travel and possibility of difficult route finding in poor weather. This area is best early in the season when the snow covers the rubble, making travel easier.

- **Wedgemount Lake:** Access is by the Wedgemount trail (page 80). Although the rock is far from the greatest, this is a popular area because of the good access and the north ridge of Wedge. This route is one of the finest snow climbs in southwestern B.C. and a must on the locals' list of classic climbs. Other climbs in the area are out-classed by it. The best time to visit is in early summer.

- **Joffre Lakes:** Approach by the Joffre Lakes trail (page 85). The finest concentration of mountaineering in the Whistler area with a bit of everything for everybody. Ice, snow, rock, easy, difficult – whatever you want is here. Four climbs stand out – the west ridge of Slalok, northwest ridge of Joffre, the north face and the east ridge of Matier – but the good rock and fine ice make everything here a treat.

It ain't all it's cracked up to be: Octopus's Garden on the Smoke Bluffs

For the visitor to this area who needs a fix of rock climbing, there is no shortage of places, as cliffs can be found anywhere along the road.

For the serious climber, however, there is only one place to go and that is the Squamish Chief (page 66), situated just south of Squamish beside Highway 99, a 45 minute drive from Whistler. It is impossible to miss – you can't hide a 500 m high granite face very easily. The Chief and the surrounding bluffs form Canada's premier rock climbing centre and one of the best in North America. This status is the result of great granite, easy access, and many types of rock climbing. There you will find everything from short climbs for beginners through the expert, easy to modern desperates, from one-pitch wonders to multi-day trials. The climbing area stretches from Murrin Park, 9 km south of the traffic lights in Squamish, to the Little Smoke Bluffs, directly across from the lights.

With over 600 routes to choose from, you really should buy a guidebook if you are going to be in the area for more than a day or two. The current guides, listed in Helpful Books, are available at Mountain Equipment Co-op in Vancouver or Extreme Mountain Gear in Squamish. If you don't have a guidebook, then try asking around the parking lot at the base of the Apron, or stroll over to the Little Smoke Bluffs (page 51).

The Apron, the expanse of 45° slabs that almost touch the road, is located on the south side of the small bridge between the traffic lights and Shannon Falls. The Apron has many excellent routes from 5.0 to 5.12. Diedre, Sparrow, and Snake are favourites. Short cracks and faces on the Smoke Bluffs offer climbs from 5.0 to 5.13; many can be top-roped. The huge, conspicuous main walls of the Squamish Chief offer a variety of long routes for the strong climber; try classics such as Grand Wall, University Wall, or Tantalus Wall.

There are two other places in the Whistler area the locals use occasionally: Cheakamus Canyon and Soo Bluffs. Neither sees much action, so they still contain vegetation and loose rock. They are worth visiting if you want to do some exploratory climbing. Reach Cheakamus Canyon by walking south from the Tantalus viewpoint (page 134) into the canyon for 30 minutes on an old hydro access road. Soo Bluffs, which are 16.6 km north of Whistler by the Green River railroad crossing, can be reached by walking along the tracks from the crossing to get to the lower bluffs. For the upper bluffs, go up the logging road that meets Highway 99 just south of the tracks for 5 km to where it crosses the Soo almost beneath the upper bluffs.

If you want a different rock climbing experience, you might try exploring the slabs 4 km north of Skookumchuck hotsprings (page 140). The rock is beautiful granite, although mossy as little climbing has occurred here, and the apres-climbing, natural hotsprings, is great. The slabs are located beside the road half a kilometre before it crosses Rogers Creek. The slabs are 75 m high and get steeper as they get higher. A lack of cracks makes the climbing serious, but there are lots of good solid belay trees. Consider taking the family and leaving them at the hotsprings while you climb. Then join them afterwards.

The Squamish-Whistler area isn't as well known for its winter ice climbing as it is for its rock climbing. Perhaps the best route, possible once every four or five years, is Shannon Falls (page 54). In the winter, Soo Bluffs (see above) have the closest frozen waterfalls to Whistler and are frequently used by the locals.

Treks

If you are in good physical condition, have extremely good wilderness skills, ability to adjust to the unexpected, and a strong adventurous streak, try some of these backpacking adventures and see some of B.C.'s most magnificent terrain. You will return from these treks with knowledge and a sense of accomplishment not easily gained any other way.

Each trip provides a different B.C. outdoor experience. The one thing they have in common is that they become more enjoyable as time passes

Mt. Garibaldi and the Névé traverse from Isosceles Pk.   Photo by Emily Butler

after you return. You will remember each for the effort required, the heavy pack, the challenge and the adventure.

All of these trips require exceptionally good wilderness skills. They all traverse remote territory, in some cases very remote. Routes are ill-defined at best. Technical climbing gear is not required, but an ice axe and rope, and the skill to use them, are good items to carry. Be sure to take a compass and the recommended topographic maps.

The route descriptions are not detailed, as anyone doing these trips must have a fair amount of experience in wilderness travel. The descriptions are intended to give access information, point out problem spots, and give you hints on the sights and sounds you will meet along the way.

A fully equipped backpack will suffice, as little more than scrambling is involved. Your party should include a couple of experienced backpackers to be sure the party can complete its journey without endangering itself. All but the Snowcap Lake trip end at a different spot than the start, so don't forget to arrange a pickup. Tell your friends when you expect to be out. Ask them to wait at least one extra day, longer if the weather has been bad, before reporting you overdue. The time estimates for these trips are average times for a competent party that doesn't loiter along the way. How long you take is entirely up to you, but spending a few extra days will allow you to enjoy the wilderness to its fullest. Of course, these extra days will also allow you to sit storms out rather hike in them.

Garibaldi Névé Traverse

Icefields . . . Mountains . . . Ski touring

The classic ski tour in southwestern B.C. This trip involves straightforward skiing across a "small" Coast Mountains icefield. It has magnificent scenery and easy skiing connecting two well known summer hiking areas. It's perfect for the intermediate skier.

Trip length: 42 km one way
Elevations: Start: 1000 m
   High point: 2100 m
   End: 700 m
Trip time: 2–3 days

Location: Between Squamish and Whistler
Maps: 92G/14 and 92G/15

Driving distance from Whistler Village:
   Start: 68.8 km (54.8 km highway, 14.0 km gravel)
   End: 27.0 km

Driving instructions: From Whistler Village, drive south on Highway 99.
   Start: This route starts at the Diamond Head parking lot, which is reached by turning at the sign in Squamish, 52.8 km from Whistler Village. Follow the paved road for 2 km, then the narrow gravel logging road for 14 km to the parking lot.
   End: The end point is at the Black Tusk parking lot, which is well marked on the left hand side of the road 24.6 km from Whistler.

Difficulty: Mostly easy but there are extended moderate sections requiring the ability to turn.

Suitability: Intermediate skiers with the guidance of an experienced backcountry skier. Trip involves glacier travel.

 Hiking: Good hiking at both Diamond Head and Black Tusk.

Cross-country skiing: Good skiing of moderate technical difficulty requiring skins. A leader experienced in glacier travel and route-finding is required.

 Climbing: Fine winter climbing on Mt. Garibaldi. Access to the Sphinx group in the spring.

 Natural wonders: Glaciers, mountains, icefields.

This is probably the closest thing B.C. has to a European-style Haute Route. With a cabin at the Elfin Lakes and a shelter at Battleship Islands, it makes a very pleasant spring ski-tour. In fact, because of the crossing of Garibaldi Lake, spring is about the only time this traverse can be done and called pleasant. The trip is done from Diamond Head to Black Tusk rather than vice-versa so as to have a net loss of elevation and to have the strenuous parts at the beginning.

From the Diamond Head parking lot the route follows the Diamond Head trail (page 69) to the cabin at Elfin Lakes. The first two-thirds of this section is a steady uphill climb to the top of Paul Ridge. From the ridge top it is slightly downhill to the cabin at Elfin Lakes. As the route to here is a popular day-outing for beginning skiers, the path is often well-worn and is well marked. From the cabin the route heads downhill to a low point that is the campground in the summer, before turning right and heading towards the Garibaldi Névé. Here the route does a descending traverse underneath avalanche-prone slopes of the Gargoyles into the Ring Creek valley. Once you reach the creek, cross to the east side and pick a route up to the Névé. Crossing Ring Creek can be a problem in late spring, as the Ring Creek bridge is removed for the winter and not replaced until after high water. It is a good idea to stay close to the edge of the bench that is above the incised river bed in order to keep away from the slopes of Opal Cone.

Gain the névé and rest after the climb, which will have taken two or three hours from the cabin. You are now in an area of ice that is very small by the standards of the Coast Mountains but nearly as large as the Columbia Icefields, the largest in the Rockies. Between the wars the Névé had an area of over 250 square kilometres. The warm period since has reduced the area covered by the ice to less than 225 square kilometres.

Head across the flat Névé towards Mt. Garibaldi and Tent Peak. Once it becomes time to climb again do an ascending traverse to the right towards some rock outcroppings at the 2100 m level. This climb is longer and steeper than it looks. On one of the outcrops there are the last remnants of a cabin. This is a great lunch stop because the view is fantastic, the strenuous part of the trip is over, and by the time you get here it will be approaching lunch time. Many parties camp here if the hour is late or the weather bad. From here five minutes of uphill and fifteen of level travel will have you overlooking the Warren Glacier. The descent route to the head of the Warren Glacier, especially the first part, contains many crevasses. Avoid these by bearing left and keeping high as you aim for the uphill side of a prominent nunatak (the Sharkfin) until a clear route down is obvious. Traverse the head of the Warren Glacier and make the gentle ascent to the col on the other side beneath Glacier Pikes, from where you get a view of Garibaldi Lake.

To reach Garibaldi Lake, bear left until forced to drop down to the Sentinel Glacier. The last part of this descent is steep and avalanche-prone on the west side but otherwise presents few problems. Before you start the descent try to spot some huts on the outcrops at the glacier's edge below; they represent the point where you reach the valley floor. Once on the valley floor a nice run leads to Garibaldi Lake. As this is about two hours from lunch and slightly less from the cabins at Battle-ship Islands it makes a good break point.

The best route across the frozen lake is to head straight for the point below Mt. Price on the left side of the lake, before heading diagonally across the lake to the cabins. The route from the cabins follows the Black Tusk trail (page 73) past the Barrier Lakes then down the Barrier trail to the parking lot. It is common practice to ski down the trail with skins on, because the first part winds in and out of the trees on a sidehill, and the second part has some extremely sharp hairpin turns and is often chewed up by people who insist on hiking in the winter. As a rule, in March it is possible to ski to within a couple of kilometres of the parking lot. The road from Highway 99 to the parking lot is not plowed but usually still covered with enough snow to justify putting your skis on for a final run.

Tundra Lake, headwater of the Stein River
Courtesy of Western Canada Wilderness Committee

Stein-Lizzie Crossover

*Large unlogged valley . . . Biogeoclimatic change . . . Alpine
meadows . . . Turquoise lakes . . . Scenery*

A long hike the length of the Stein River that takes you from the coastal
climate zone to interior climate zone. The Stein is the last major unlogged valley in southwestern B.C. and this trip gives you a chance to see
what the province looked like before logging started.

Trip length: 72 km one way

Elevations: Start:1300 m
  High point: 2100 m
  End: 300 m
Trip time: 5–9 days

Location: Between Pemberton and Lillooet
Maps: 92J/1, 92J/8, and 92I/5

Driving distance from Whistler Village:
  Start: 7.1 km (40.5 km highway, 36.6 km gravel)
  End: 193 km from Whistler to Lytton via the Duffey Lake road
  and Lillooet; 270 km from Vancouver to Lytton via Highway 1

Driving instructions:
  Start: From Whistler Village, drive 31.9 km north on Highway 99
  to Pemberton. Go right 6.6 km to the church in Mount Currie.
  Turn right and drive 10.0 km to the Lillooet Lake road. Drive
  down the road for 17.7 km and turn left up a logging road
  immediately before a bridge. Stay on the main branch for 7.9
  km then go left and right, and climb a steep hill before
  paralleling Lizzie Creek. The parking area is located at 10.9 km.
  End: Near Lytton. A ferry crosses the Fraser River 2.0 km north
  of Lytton on Highway 12. Take the ferry to the west side and
  drive 4.8 km north to a turnoff (left side). Turn and drive in 1.0
  km to the parking area.

Difficulty: Easy with moderate sections and one steep downhill.

Suitability: Anyone who can carry a heavy pack for a few hours.
  Teenagers and up. The party should be led by an experienced
  backpacker. Requires no technical gear.

Hiking: There are numerous unmarked side trips possible in the alpine regions, and a number of trails climb from the Stein valley floor back into the alpine.

 Climbing: Stiff scrambles and easy glaciated peaks are located on the south side of the valley.

 Swimming: Numerous tarns available for swimming in the alpine. Stein Lake can be swum in. The streams that enter the Stein have calm backwaters that provide safe swimming.

 Natural wonders: Glaciers, mountains, icefields, biogeoclimatic zones.

The Stein River valley is the only large valley in southwestern B.C. that remains unlogged and as such has been the subject of a major environmental battle since the early 1970s. A byproduct of this publicity has been an increased interest in the Stein as a hiking area, with the trip down the entire length of the river now being one of the classic backpacking trips of southwestern B.C.

Start the trip by hiking up the Lizzie Meadows trail and over to Tundra Lake (page 88). From the west end of Tundra circle the lake on its northern side, staying above the cliffs that drop straight into the lake. At the eastern end you are at the edge of a hanging valley looking down, a long way down, to Stein Lake. From here the route traverses scree on the north side of the valley without any change in elevation until the rocks from the ridge meet your traverse line. Clamber up the rocks and continue along the ridge crest until you see Poppet Lake 150 m below you.

From Poppet Lake you can continue along the ridge to the east end of Stein Lake then head down. Alternatively, stay on the east side of the creek that flows out of Poppet Lake and head straight down to the west end of Stein Lake, where a bushy trail runs along the shore to the log jam at the far end. Cross the log jam and pick up the well-marked trail that will take you the rest of the way to the mouth of the Stein near Lytton.

If you have the time, you will do well to spend a day hiking up to Elton Lake, reached by heading up the ridge on the other side of the log jam. This lake is a gem, with a glacier descending right into the deepest and truest turquoise water that you will ever see.

As you hike down to the mouth of the river through this unlogged valley, remember it is the only major unlogged valley in this portion of the province, and one of very few in the south half of the province. Think of what it says about our society, and the forestry industry in particular, that we are even considering logging this valley. Of all the arguments for not logging the Stein valley, and most are extremely persuasive, the simplest and most understandable, or clearcut if you will excuse the pun, is "Do we have to log absolutely every last valley in the region, province, country, or the world?" An increasing large number of people now answer "No!" This not to say we shouldn't log – after all this book would not exist without logging – but we should do it with care, respect, and proper ecological practices. That care includes the complete preservation of some valleys, and in southwestern B.C. the only one we have left is the Stein valley. That's what makes it so precious, as you will probably agree after this trip.

As you continue down the valley past Stein Lake, you will notice a gradual change in tree cover as the area becomes drier. Cedars and hemlocks give way to Ponderosa pines, which tolerate the drier conditions better. The forest become more open and there is less underbrush beside the trail. You will cross the Stein River three times, including once in a little cable car. This crossing will give you an exhilarating swoop across the water and the desire to be a kid and do it a second time. After at least three days of gentle hiking you will emerge onto the Lytton Indian Reserve a short distance from the Fraser River. Turn right on the road to reach the ferry across the Fraser to Lytton, where you can be picked up or catch a bus back to Vancouver.

The hike down the Stein offers so much to see and do that you really should invest in a Stein valley guidebook before you go (see Helpful Books).

Two Goat Ridge

Views ... Glaciers ... Tarns ... Lakes ... Scenery ... Mountain scrambling

A high ridge scramble on the crest of the Coast Mountains. Views west to the icefields and eastward to the interior alpine ridges. The route involves alpine scrambling and passes three turquoise lakes and two high mountain tarns. The wide ridge is located 2000 m above Lillooet Lake and provides unbelievable views of the Pemberton Valley.

Trip length: 22 km one way
Elevations: Start: 1280 m
   High point: 2380 m
   End: 200 m
Trip time: 14 hours; overnight

Location: Immediately above the east side of Lillooet Lake
Maps: 92J/7 and 92J/8

Driving distance from Whistler Village:
   Start: 61.1 km (52.1 km highway, 9 km gravel road)
   End: 57.5 km (39.5 km highway, 18.0 km gravel road)

Driving instructions: From Whistler Village, drive 31.9 km north to Pemberton. Go right 6.6 km to the church in Mount Currie.
   Start: Turn right on the Duffey Lake road and drive 24 km to Joffre Lakes Recreation Area (signposted). Start up Joffre Lakes trail.
   End: For pickup, drive 10 km down the Duffey Lake road from Mount Currie and take the right fork down Lillooet Lake. Route exits onto Lillooet Lake road at 9.0 km. Twin One campsite is 0.7 km to the south.

Difficulty: Stiff scrambling.

Suitability: Anyone who is comfortable doing easy rock climbing and is fairly fit.

Hiking: Easy hiking up to Upper Joffre Lake but after the lake it is a stiff scramble for expert hikers only.

 Climbing: The Joffre area has one of the finest concentrations of rugged alpine peaks in this region.

 Swimming: It is theoretically possible to swim in the lakes, but they are for penguins only. The tarns on the ridge provide very enjoyable swimming in the late summer.

 Natural wonders: Glaciers, mountains, icefields.

If you want a summer trip that provides entertainment with a physical workout in a unbelievable setting surrounded by magnificent views, then this the tour for you.

Start by hiking up the Joffre Lakes trail (page 85) to the picnic area where Tszil Creek enters the upper lake. From here, follow Tszil Creek to the col at its head by staying on the left side until you get above the trees, then switch to the right for the final ascent to the col. At the col turn left and ascend the ridge to the summit of Tszil. The ridge is sprinkled with small bluffs that may be climbed directly or avoided by bearing slightly left. From the summit descend to the col between Tszil and Slalok, then go down the scree slope to Two Goat tarn. The tarn is a nice camping spot, highly swimmable, and the last year-round water source actually on the route. From the tarn ascend the scree to gain Two Goat Ridge, which joins Slalok to Duffey Peak. The ridge is obvious and, like the rest of the route, is broken by the occasional small rock bluff. There is no problem in getting around these bluffs, but care should be taken. The ascent to the top of Duffey Peak is an easy scramble. From the summit you get magnificent views of Lillooet Lake and the Pemberton Valley over two vertical kilometres below, and the surrounding mountains and icefields.

As you sit on Duffey Peak gazing at one of the world's great mountain vistas, you are also sitting on the crest of the Coast Mountains, or Coast Range as they are often called. This position enables you to see the two distinct sides of the Coast Range, the wet western side and the dry eastern side, and the broad biogeoclimatic zones that are the result. As you look across Lillooet Lake into Garibaldi Park your view is dominated by coniferous forests and icefields that are the result of the heavy precipitation that occurs when the clouds rise to cross the mountains as they come in off the Pacific Ocean. A look eastward, back in the direction from whence you came, shows the effect of being on the lee side of the mountains. Here a dry environment with fewer coniferous trees and ice-fields is the result of the clouds having dumped most of their moisture on the windward side.

Head south from the summit, descending the ridge just to the left side of the crest. A hundred metres below the col between Duffey Peak and the second summit there is Drop-Off Tarn, which makes an ideal camping or lunch spot. It is also the last year round water supply until you are a matter of minutes from the logging roads. The ascent to the second peak can be accomplished by either ascending the ridge directly, climbers only, or scrambling up the scree on the right side. From this peak descend the left side of the ridge, then hike up the right side of the final peak. When you reach the top of this last summit, take a final break on the farther of the two peaks and have a look at the route down.

Now for a knee-bashing descent of 2000 m. Although descending in any direction will get you down, the best way is to aim for the point where Twin One Creek enters Lillooet Lake. Follow the ridge that descends towards the lake. As you start to reach the edge of the alpine zone, drop left in a scree bowl that becomes a gully. The gully starts as a scree slope then becomes a vegetated creek bed that is generally dry. Because of the vegetation you might want to wear long pants and a shirt in this bottom section. The creek bed falls steadily and steeply but there are no cliffs to worry about. The creek finally pops out into the logging slash at about the 800 m level. Turn right and follow the road downhill to where it joins the Lillooet Lake road. If someone is going to pick you up, have them wait at the Twin One forestry campsite, which you can reach by turning left on the Lillooet Lake road. Just tell your friend to have dinner ready for you.

Snowcap Lake

Glaciers descending into the lake . . . Icebergs . . . Icefields . . .
Moutain scrambling

This is a rugged trip suitable only for the fit backpacker. The party leader should have extensive off-trail wilderness experience. At your destination you will find a lake backdropped by an icefield that has to be seen as it is impossible to describe.

Trip length: 20 km one way
Elevations: Start: 150 m
   High point: 2375 m (Mt. Greenmantle)
   End: 1400 m
Trip time: 2–3 days (each way)

Location: On the eastern side of Garibaldi Park, due west of
   Skookumchuck village.
Maps: 92G/15 and 92G/16

Driving distance from Whistler Village: 91.7 km
   39.4 km highway
   52.3 km gravel

Driving instructions: From Whistler Village, drive 31.9 km north on
   Highway 99. Go right at T-junction. Drive 6.6 km to the Duffey
   Lake road turnoff, then 10.0 km to the Lillooet Lake road
   turnoff. Drive down the east side road for 29.0 km to the Tenas
   Lake bridge. Cross to the west side road and go down it for 24.3
   km. Park off-road on an old logging road.

Difficulty: Some moderate rock climbing, and a short section of
   glacier travel.

Suitability: Good for the experienced backpacker who has done
   some rock scrambling and has extensive off-trail experience.
   Take ice axes and a climbing rope.

Hiking: Limited easy hiking at Snowcap Lake. Good alpine meadow rambling on Icemantle Koli7.

 Climbing: Easy climbing on glaciers.

Swimming: Tarns on Icemantle Koli7 and at eastern end of Snowcap Lake.

If Snowcap Lake were accessible by car, tourists would be flocking to it like they do to Lake Louise and the Columbia Icefield. The southern edge of the lake is fringed with glaciers from the Snowcap Icefield beyond. At least one glacier reaches into the lake. The northern edge is formed by the steep flanks of Mt. Greenmantle, and the magnificent sentinel of Mt. Pitt casts its reflection into the lake from the western edge. If you want to see the glory of the Coast Mountains in all their many forms then this is an ideal trip.

The route to Snowcap Lake starts by climbing the slopes above the west Lillooet River road between Tuwasus Creek and Glacier Creek. Although heading anywhere up the hillside will get you onto the ridge that takes you to the Icemantle Koli7 (pronounced col-eh), the best starting spot is at kilometre 24.3, where you can hike up an old logging road to ease your ascent and eliminate some of the bushwacking on this incredibly steep slope. Where the road forks, go right. From the end of the road, head up the hill until you reach the ridge crest. This will take 6 hours from the main road. Because the ridge ends in a bump you will have to lose some altitude as you walk southwest towards the Icemantle Koli7. Koli7 is a Lil'wat word, the Indians inhabiting this area, that means green and/or yellow (there is no differentiation in their language between these two colours) but it is also used to mean alpine meadows.

Once on the Koli7 head across it bearing slightly to the right aiming to reach the far side of it. This meadow is immense: about 4 km across. From the back right corner drop a short distance down the Glacier Lake side to a watercourse and follow it back to a lake in a cirque. The cirque has a wall at its back that is shown on the topographical map as being very steep. It isn't – it's vertical. Ascend the ridge on the south side of the Icemantle Glacier to the summit of Three Bears Mountain. Traverse the peak. The west ridge involves descending class 3 and 4 rock for about 200 m but there are lots of good holds. Climb Mt. Greenmantle by ascending

Looking south from Greenmantle to your camping area by the moraine

the east face on easy ledges. It is easy to find a route up but it is very tricky to pick out the easiest route on the return from above. From the summit of Greenmantle continue westward along the ridge crest until you see a draw that takes you down to Snowcap Lake. It is a long steep descent, 500 vertical metres, to the lakeshore. When you reach the lakeshore work your way around the edge to the gravel benches on the far side. Allow two long days to reach the lake and the same to get out.

It is worth spending a few days exploring the area around the lake. Consider spending the first day lying in the many tarns that are located just southeast of Snowcap Lake recovering from your trip in. On another day you might try walking along the lake's edge, more correctly lakes, just to savour the views. Go along the southern slope of the upper lake toward the spit that separates the lakes. There is a tricky piece of route-finding through the rock promontory at the west end of the upper lake. Just beyond the promontory you can walk out on the spit and cross the 5-m-wide creek joining the two lakes that make up Snowcap Lake to get to the lower lake's north side. It is worth getting your feet cold to get the great view of the Thundercap Glacier descending into the lower lake. The outlet from this lake is an unbelievable box canyon that is something to see. If you have a rope and ice axe climb up the glaciers on the south side of the lake and look out over the Snowcap and Misty icefields.

Having done some or all of these things you now have the pleasure of retracing your route in. Have fun packing up the slopes of Greenmantle. The route involves a lot of sweating but it's well worth it, and given half a chance you'll be back.

There is a tremendous feeling that comes on trip like this, with so much to see, and so much to do and all of it unknown. Have you ever taken a dog on a hike? Well, imagine yourself as the dog. As a dog you don't have worry about the weather or the route; the details of the hike are not concerns of yours; your only concern is to swim in every tarn, climb over every rock and experience every moment of this mysterious hike that you are being taken on. But who, you might ask, is taking you on the hike? The mountains! Who else lays out the route? Who else decides when it is sunny and when it rains? And who else do you sidle up to panting, hot and exhausted?

John Baldwin
Canadian Alpine Journal, 1989

Warner Pass

Interior backpacking... Gentle alpine terrain... Pocket
glaciers... Meadows

This is an easy and straightforward backpack in eye-popping terrain on
the interior side of the Coast Mountains. The start at high elevation, easy
access to spectacular alpine meadows, and generally good weather make
this a memorable and popular trip.

Trip length: 70 km one way
Elevations: Start: 1325 m
   High point: 2390 m
   End: 1125 m
Trip time: 4–7 days

Location: Between Taseko Lakes and Gold Bridge, northeast of
   Whistler and southwest of Williams Lake.
Maps: 92O/3, 92O/4, 92J/15. 92O/2 and 92J/14 are also useful.

Access: Fly into Taseko Lakes from Whistler by floatplane, or take
   Highway 20 west from Williams Lake to Hanceville and go south
   on logging roads to Taseko Lakes.
   Fly out from Spruce Lake or get picked up at the Jewel Creek
   bridge. The latter is reached by driving to Gold Bridge and going
   up to Gun Lake. There is an obscure logging road coming in
   from the left side 14.0 km from the Bailey bridge in Gold Bridge.
   Go up the road for 0.9 km and turn left. Take the right hand
   forks until 22.1 km from Gold Bridge where a parking lot off to
   the right side marks the location of the bridge.

Difficulty: Easy with short moderate sections.

Suitability: Anyone who can carry a heavy pack for a few hours
   each day. Good for teenagers and adults. The party should be
   led by an experienced backpacker. Requires no technical gear.

Hiking: Gentle hiking with lots of side trip possibilities.

 Swimming: Lakes, tarns and small rivers.

 Fishing: Good fishing for rainbow in Warner, Trigger, Hummingbird and Spruce lakes.

 Natural wonders: Alpine flowers galore.

If you want to take your older children on a backpack, or if you want a change of scenery from the rugged terrain near Whistler, then give Warner Pass a whirl. It's one of the finest hikes in the province. Although not strictly in the Whistler area, you can easily reach it from Whistler by flying from Green Lake. The route goes southward from Taseko Lakes on an old mining road until just past Battlement Creek, then it follows a horse trail up and over Warner Pass to the Jewel Creek bridge.

The route offers a good physical geography lesson. Few people in the province know that B.C. is not one vast mountain range, and fewer still know that in the south the mountain ranges are limited to the eastern and western sides of the province while the central part is a series of plateaus. The Warner Pass journey walks the boundary between the Coast Mountains and Chilcotin Plateau to the east and shows the characteristics of an area in transition. Being in the rain shadow of the Coast Mountains, the most obvious difference between Warner Pass and Whistler is in the amount of rainfall. The Chilcotin Plateau and Warner Pass have low average rainfall because they are sheltered from the prevailing rain-bearing winds by a range of mountains. Another difference is the gentler nature of the landscape, caused by the difference in elevation between the valley floor and mountain tops being considerably less than near the coast. Taseko Lakes, where this trip starts, is at 1325 m elevation, about twice the altitude of Whistler Village, yet the mountain peaks are about the same height.

From the south end of the upper Taseko Lake head up the Taseko River valley on an old mining road. The road starts by climbing steeply up and over the canyon on the Taseko River. There are good views of the canyon about two-thirds of the way up the climb. Here the Taseko River has cut down through the soft rock that blocks its path to Taseko Lakes. At the top of the climb, about two hours up, is Summit Lake. While the water is warm and very swimmable, the bottom of the lake is a deep layer of organic matter into which you will sink slowly (watch for leeches!). This trait is common in lakes that form in dips in the rocks. Organic matter falls in and rots into soil that will eventually turns the lake into a marsh, then a quaking or floating bog, a bog, and finally a meadow. From here the road flattens out and rolls along the valley floor to a ford at Battlement Creek. This is the second creek you cross and is easily recognizable by the rusty colour which it gets from the mineral deposits in the mountains above. A short distance beyond the ford the road starts to climb steeply; here take the very old road that forks to the right down to the Taseko River. After a half kilometre the road ends and the trail begins.

For an hour the trail winds along the valley floor to Denain Creek, the first large creek you meet. Although there is a blaze visible on the other side, don't cross here. Instead the route swings up the river and heads to the alpine. This part of the trail, from Battlement Creek to the alpine, is characterized by a large number of old horse trails and trap lines; consequently it is festooned with blazes and trails that just end. If you lose the trail, just keep parallel to the Taseko until you reach the Denain and then head uphill. As you go uphill your path will be interrupted by the Feo Creek canyon. Wander along the canyon edge until you see a horse trail on the opposite side; the crossing is below. As you approach the alpine, it is easy to lose the trail again. To re-find it, stay on the bench about 100 m above the river. There are some great camping sites as you enter the alpine. The best is at a tarn on the upper edge of the meadows. It's right by the trail and impossible to miss.

From Warner Pass an easy-to-follow trail leads all the way to the pickup points. The trail starts by descending the talus in a small hanging valley. From the edge of the valley you make a descending traverse through the subalpine to Warner Lake. There is a good camping spot immediately after crossing a small creek a couple of hundred metres before the lake. From here follow the edge of Warner Lake, then Gun Creek, before dropping steeply just before arriving at the Trigger Lake cabin, which is open to the public. This lovely cabin is used by packtrains on their way to the many parts of the Chilcotin Plateau that are accessible from here. Twenty minutes beyond the cabin you reach Trigger Lake. Follow the shoreline and then Gun Creek to Hummingbird Lake and a campsite at the far end. From Hummingbird the trail continues down Gun Creek to a marked fork leading to Spruce Lake. Here in the aspen groves that grace this part of the trail you have the choice of going 3 km up to Spruce Lake for a pre-arranged flight home, or continuing down the valley for 14 km to the Jewel Creek bridge and a vehicle pick-up.

Trip Ideas

Want to do something with the kids? Take a day off from downhill skiing? Interested in birds? Here are some especially good trips, arranged thematically in no particular order.

Families with Very Young Children
Lillooet River dikes 58
Alice Lake 49
Brandywine Falls 46
Shannon Falls 54
Lost Lake 36

Families with Children
Squamish Chief 66
Joffre Lakes 85
Alpine Blackcomb 39
B.C. Railway 154
Nairn Falls 56
River of Golden Dreams 114

Families with Teenagers
Warner Pass 189
Singing Pass 77
Black Tusk 73
Diamond Head 69
Rainbow Lake 83
Lizzie Meadows 88
Soo River logging road 107

The Elderly
Shannon Falls 54
Brandywine Falls 46
Lost Lake 36
Cougar Mountain 41

Hate Exercise?
Brandywine Falls 46
Meager Creek hotsprings 138
Skookumchuck church &
    hotsprings 147
B.C. Railway 154
Duffy-Hurley Circuit 149

Great Scenery
Black Tusk 73
Diamond Head 69
Snowcap Lake 185
Two Goat Ridge 182

Warner Pass 189
Tantalus viewpoint 134
Joffre Lakes 85
Singing Pass 77

Waterfalls
Callaghan Lake (Alexander
    Falls) 97
Brandywine Falls 46
Shannon Falls 54
Nairn Falls 56

Mountain Lakes
Joffre Lakes 85
Snowcap Lake 185
Black Tusk 73
Wedgemount Lake 80
Lizzie Meadows 88
Taseko Lakes flight 158

Glaciers
Wedgemount Lake 80
Snowcap Lake 185
Tantalus viewpoint 134
Garibaldi Névé traverse 175
Snekwnukwa7 Glacier 109

Volcanic Features
Diamond Head 69
Black Tusk 73
Taseko Lakes flight 158
Garibaldi Névé traverse 175

Biogeoclimatic Zones
B.C. Railway 154
Duffey-Hurley circuit 149
Two Goat Ridge 182
Stein-Lizzie crossover 179

Alpine Meadows and Flowers
Black Tusk 73
Singing Pass 77
Lizzie Meadows 88
Warner Pass 189

Bird Watching
Birkenhead River & Lake 123, 132
Four Lakes walk 49
One Mile Lake 56
Lillooet River dikes 58

Big Trees
Cheakamus Lake 44
Cougar Mountain 41

History
Skookumchuck church 147
Harrison-Lillooet Trail 144
B.C. Railway 154
Duffey-Hurley circuit 149

Winter Walks
Four Lakes walk 49
Lillooet River dikes 58
Lillooet Lake walks 61
Sloquet Hotsprings 142
Nairn Falls & One Mile Lake 56

Spring Hikes
Squamish Chief 66
Singing Pass 77
Lost Lake 36
Birkenhead Lake 132

Fall Hikes
Blowdown Creek 107
Van Horlick Creek 107
Valley Trail 93
Cheakamus Lake 44

Flat Bike Rides
Valley Trail 93
Upper Pemberton Valley 96

Rolling Bike Rides
Pemberton-D'Arcy 96
Rutherford Creek 107
Soo River 107

Early Winter Cross-country Skiing
Van Horlick Creek 107
Blowdown Creek 107
Diamond Head 69

Late Winter Cross-country Skiing
Singing Pass 77
Snekwnukwa7 Glacier 109
Garibaldi Névé traverse 175

Lake Canoeing
One Mile Lake 56
Alice Lake 49
Alta and Green lakes 115

Gentle River Canoeing
Middle Lillooet River 116
River of Golden Dreams 114

Kayaking
Upper Lillooet River 119
Cheakamus River 121
Birkenhead River 123

Family Fishing
Callaghan Lake 97, 128
Cheakamus River 121, 129
Birkenhead River 123, 128
Alice Lake 49, 128

Rainy Day Trips
Hotsprings 136
Skookumchuck church 147
Duffey-Hurley circuit 149
B.C. Railway 154
Cougar Mountain 41

Extremely Hot Day Trips
Swimming holes 131
Cheakamus Lake 44
River of Golden Dreams 114
Middle Lillooet River 116
Birkenhead River 123

Car Camping
Lillooet Lake walks 61
Meager Creek hotsprings 138
Callaghan Lake 97
Nairn Falls 56
Birkenhead Lake 132
Alice Lake 49

Easy Overnight
Lizzie Meadows 88
Joffre Lakes 85
Blowdown Creek 107
Black Tusk 73
Diamond Head 69

Physical Workout
Wedgemount Lake 80
Snekwnukwa7 Glacier 109
Snowcap Lake 185

Helpful Books

The following is a selection of the current guidebooks that have useful information on the Whistler area. Some are a bit dated and some are better than others. No guide, this one included, should be taken as the last word and all are out-dated as soon as they are published!

Armstrong, John. *Vancouver Geology*. 1990, third edition. Vancouver: Geological Association of Canada, Cordilleran Section. Good, non-technical account of the geology between Vancouver and Squamish. Much is applicable to the Whistler area.

Burbridge, Joan. *Wildflowers of the Southern Interior of British Columbia and adjacent parts of Washington, Idaho, and Montana*. 1989. Vancouver: UBC Press. Very attractive, easy-to-use guide, useful for the Lillooet, Gold Bridge, and alpine areas.

Campbell, Jim. *Squamish Rock Climbs*. 1991. Vancouver: the author. A topo guide, particularly good for the Smoke Bluffs area.

Christie, Jack. *Day Trips from Vancouver*. 1989. Vancouver: Brighouse Press. A guide to activities within a day's drive of Vancouver.

Coo, Bill. *Scenic Rail Guide to Western Canada*. 1985 revised edition. Toronto: Greey de Pencier Books. Summarizes the sights along the B.C. Railway.

Coward, Garth. *Tree Book: Learning to Recognize Trees of British Columbia*. 1992. Victoria: British Columbia Ministry of Forests and Forestry Canada. A superb guide to the trees of B.C., available free from the Ministry of Forests in Victoria. Simple to use and full of useful information.

Decker, Frances, Margaret Fouberg, and Mary Ronayne. *Pemberton: The History of a Settlement*. 1977. Pemberton: Pemberton Pioneer Women. History of European settlement in the Pemberton Valley.

Fairley, Bruce. *A Guide to Climbing and Hiking in Southwestern British Columbia*. 1986. Vancouver: Gordon Soules. Excellent climbing guide to southwestern B.C.

Graydon, Don, Ed. *Mountaineering: The Freedom of the Hills*. 1992, fifth edition. Seattle: The Mountaineers. The bible for climbers and wilderness travellers in the Coast Mountains.

Lyons, C. P. *Trees, Shrubs & Flowers to Know in British Columbia*. 1965. Vancouver: J. M. Dent & Sons. An oldie but goodie. Ideal for the beginner as it covers the common plants in an easy to understand fashion.

Macaree, Mary and David. *103 Hikes in Southwestern British Columbia.* 1987, third edition. Vancouver: Douglas and McIntyre; Seattle: The Mountaineers. Guide to selected non-technical trails and routes in the Lower Mainland.

Macaree, Mary and David. *109 Walks in Southwestern British Columbia.* 1990, third edition. Vancouver: Douglas and McIntyre; Seattle: The Mountaineers. Comprehensive guide to easy walks in southwestern B.C.

MacKinnon, Andy, Jim Pojar, and Ray Coupé. *Plants of Northern British Columbia.* 1992. Edmonton: Lone Pine Publishing. Although intended for the area somewhat north of the Whistler area, this is the best guide to the plants (trees, shrubs, grasses, lichens, ferns) under one cover there is, especially for the subalpine and alpine regions of this area. It is worth the investment even if you never go to northern B.C.

Mathews, W.H. *Garibaldi Geology.* 1975. Vancouver: Geological Association of Canada, Cordilleran Section. Excellent non-technical account of the geology of Garibaldi Park, especially good for the volcanic features in the area.

McDonald, Jim. *Hotsprings of Western Canada.* 1991. Vancouver: Waterwheel Press. A reissue of an older guide. Useful but access routes and descriptions are badly dated (1970s). Look for an all-new guide in 1994.

McLane, Kevin. *The Rockclimbers' Guide to Squamish.* 1992. Squamish: Merlin Productions. A superb guide to the Squamish Chief and the area stretching from Vancouver to Pemberton.

Ministry of the Environment. *British Columbia Recreational Atlas.* 1989. Victoria: Government of B.C. A detailed road atlas of B.C.

Okay Anglers. *B.C. Fishing Directory and Atlas.* Port Coquitlam: Art Belhumeur Enterprises. Maps, information, and articles. Updated annually.

Page, Jay, Alan Dibb, Paul Phillips, and Bruce Blackwell. *A Guide to Ski Touring in the Whistler, Garibaldi, Squamish, and Pemberton Areas.* 1984. Vancouver: Varsity Outdoor Club. Particularly good for Garibaldi Park.

Peterson, Roger Tory. *A field guide to western birds: a completely new guide to field marks of all species found in North America west of the 100th meridian and north of Mexico.* 1990, third edition. Boston: Houghton Mifflin. A standard field guide, useful throughout B.C.

Pratt-Johnson, Betty. *Whitewater Trips for Kayakers, Canoeists and Rafters in British Columbia: Greater Vancouver through Whistler, Okanagan and Thompson River Regions.* 1986. Vancouver: Adventure Publishing: Seattle: Pacific Search Press. Includes about 10 trips in the Whistler area.

Priest, Simon. *Bicycling Southwest British Columbia & The Sunshine Coast.* 1985. Vancouver: Douglas & McIntyre. A guide and mileage chart to southwestern B.C.

Selters, Andy. *Glacier Travel and Crevasse Rescue.* 1990. Seattle: The Mountaineers. A great resource for anyone planning to travel on glaciers.

Stoltmann, Randy. *Hiking Guide to the Big Trees of Southwestern British Columbia.* 1990, second edition. Vancouver: Western Canada Wilderness Committee. A fantastic guide to some of nature's greatest wonders.

Udvardy, Miklos D.F. *The Audubon Society Field Guide to North American Birds: Western Region.* 1984. New York: Alfred A. Knopf. Getting dated, but still useful and very popular.

Vitt, Dale H., Janet E. Marsh, and Robin B. Bovey. *Mosses, Lichens & Ferns of Northwest North America.* 1988. Edmonton: Lone Pine Publishing. Everything you need to know about mosses, ferns and lichens. A great book for identification freaks!

Wareham, Bill. *British Columbia Wildlife Viewing Guide.* 1991. Edmonton: Lone Pine Publishing. A superb guide to the important wildlife areas of B.C. Well presented and easy to read.

White, Gordon. *Stein Valley Wilderness Guidebook.* 1991. Vancouver: Stein Wilderness Alliance. An excellent guidebook to the Stein and Duffey Lake area. The superb introduction has much on the natural history of the region.

Whitney, Stephen. *The Audubon Society Nature Guides: Western Forests.* 1985. New York: Alfred A Knopf. A fine field guide to the forests on the west coast of North America.

Whitney, Stephen. *A Field Guide to the West Coast Mountains.* 1983 Vancouver: Douglas and McIntyre; Seattle: The Mountaineers. An excellent natural history of the Cascades, Coast Mountains, Vancouver Island and the Olympics.

Index

The main trips and the page on which they are described are in bold.